COMPLEXITIES
OF
ECSTASY

Debunking
the Taboo Nature of
Conversations about Sex

JOCELYN M. KIRKLAND

CONTENTS

Acknowledgments   1
Introduction   5

PART I: WE DON'T TALK ABOUT SEX ENOUGH!

Chapter 1: Penetrating Silence   13
Chapter 2: Fauxgasms and Such...   27
Chapter 3: As Seen on TV...   39
Part I: Conversation Corner   53

PART II: WE SHOULD TALK ABOUT SEX MORE!

Chapter 4: Blissful Ignorance   57
Chapter 5: Is this Normal?   67
Chapter 6: Twisted Minds and Their Trails of   89
Residue...
Part II: Conversation Corner   106

PART III: WHEN WE START TO TALK ABOUT SEX...

Chapter 7: Turn ons and Turn offs   111
Chapter 8: Sensuality   117
Chapter 9: Beyond Your Wildest Dreams   129
Part III: Conversation Corner   142

Appendix   145

This book is dedicated to every woman empowered by God to formulate her thoughts and feelings to write her sex story. My sincere prayer is that your pen never runs dry, and you are encouraged to speak, think, and engage in fruitful conversations that enhance your very life in every way possible.

ACKNOWLEDGMENTS

First off, I just want to mention that acknowledging anyone makes me extremely nervous because I'm 100% sure I'm going to leave people out that deserve credit for their contributions to my life and specifically to this book. I love very hard and there are so many people I must thank. From random conversations to official interviews, every single event contributed to the composition of this book. If you're reading these words right now...thank you! Your attention in this moment is more than I could even ask for, and I pray that the words printed on these pages count as time and attention well spent.

To my dear husband, Jonathan Kirkland, who has selflessly and relentlessly poured out his love and support to me in all my endeavors. Babe, you have enhanced my life and perspective in ways beyond what I could've ever imagined or prayed for. From the silent moments to hours of thoughtful conversation, you push me forward and water my roots. Your words, hugs, prayer, sex and everything else make my life richer. I love you Boo! Seeing you pursue your hopes and dreams and walking in this life with you has shattered every doubt that could potentially stop me. Hard work and dreaming is what we do! Life is fun with you! I've enjoyed all of the "research" we poured into this thing, and I plan to continue our "research" as time goes on. Thank you for sharing the spotlight and being the wind beneath my wings. If this is a support competition I humbly admit you're giving me a run for my money. I love you and will always cherish what we share.

To my babies, Joy and Jada, everything I do is for you. You are the result of some of the best sex I've had, you're literally a product of the topic of this book. I'm grateful! All jokes aside, this is my first book and it's significant because we will be able to take it and sit it beside the books to come and acknowledge God's hand in my growth. Any time you get fearful or doubt who you are or what you have, you'll be reminded that you are and have more than enough right now! I don't know how you all will feel about having the "sex book mom", but I'm sure you'll be ok. Moms are supposed to be embarrassing at some point. Right?

Special thanks to my parents, David and Angela Elmore, who birthed, raised, and commanded me to take this world by storm. You birthed an author and revolutionary long before my first word was ever even uttered, let alone written/typed. Your love story cultivated me as a storyteller and a writer, and I'll continue to compose as long as I'm here. You're the best parents ever! Thank you for not clipping my wings and instead teaching me how to use them.

To my big brother, David, who has always protected, encouraged, and demonstrated what a champion truly looks like. When presented with the idea of this book, you immediately demanded that I sell you my first 10 copies. You're kind of a bully, but I love that kind of bullying! I was so excited! I was proud! I hadn't even finished writing yet, but you were down for me! You always have been. You may not know it but I think every writer's fear at some point is if people will actually buy their work. You zapped that idea out of my mind because I had already sold 10 copies so in my mind I was validated. Thank you for always believing in me always!

To my sisters in love, LaTasha and Ava, God saw fit to bless me with sisters in my adult years, and he was right on time. You both teach, encourage and uplift me in ways that I couldn't have asked for. God allowed you all to be chosen just for me (forget the brothers. lol) Thank you for living out true sisterhood with me. You both protect me in ways that no one would ever know. Being your little sister is an honor and privilege that I don't take lightly. I look up to you both!

To my Parents in-love, Charles and Glenda Kirkland, you genetically produced a masterpiece when you made my husband. Thanks! Your "connection" created the recipient of my affection and I'm grateful for it! I appreciate your love, acceptance and support throughout the years. I'm glad to have you in my life and be a part of yours.

To my brothers in love, Marcus and Charles, thanks for always having my back and loving on me as your little sister. To my nieces, Logan and Lori, and nephew David, Auntie Jossie loves you tremendously. To my Godchildren, always follow your dreams! Nothing is impossible and don't allow anything to stop you from accomplishing your goals.

To my BFF, Elizabeth, you are a constant reminder of God's preservation and love, and I'm so grateful for the bond we have. Your boldness, courage and perseverance are a miracle to behold. I'm honored to know you and to be able to witness you live out God's grace in the ways you have. I love you Sister!

To my God mommy Pat, A.K.A. "Nana," thank you for always making me feel like a priority. You are a living, breathing reminder to "keep it moving" no matter what and that motivates me more than you know. You are thoughtful and selfless always and I can depend on thoughts of you to maintain a Godly posture when it comes to loving on others.

To my Virtual Kickbacks family, thank you for your commitment and encouragement. You guys would often give me the push that I didn't know I needed. To my editor, Kierra James, and the House Capacity Publishing Team, thank you for your patience and diligence in helping me to make this book all that I hoped it could be. To my writing mentor, Shawn T. Blanchard, thank you for patiently walking this thing out with me. Your words, encouragement, and resources made this all come together in ways that I wasn't sure were possible.

Again, to every single person who has loved, supported, and believed in me, this book is for you. Thank you for your unyielding love and support. It's because of you that I am! May this book positively impact this world in ways I can't imagine.

INTRODUCTION

I'm sitting in front of my laptop with a goofy grin and a hesitant gaze. Am I really about to do what I'm planning to? Me? Little ole me? The thought of writing an entire book about conversations concerning sex or anything sex related feels weird...prohibited even...but absolutely necessary. How did I get here, you ask? Well, I sat and reflected on my own sexual journey and realized there was a lot that I didn't know, couldn't say and refused to entertain very early in my journey. Clouded by thoughts, expectations and ideas that I didn't even realize were there, I did what I thought I was "supposed" to do. I'm going to be very transparent and vulnerable here, and I ask that you brace yourself. I was a married, sexually active adult that had never experienced an orgasm and couldn't begin to explain why nor seek help to fix it. Now, that may be a shocker to some and a familiar confession to others, however; I wanted to plainly lead with that confession because that is no longer my story, but the thought that it could be, inspired me to birth this book.

Various thoughts and feelings of frustration, embarrassment, disappointment and despair danced around in my subconscious and conscious thoughts and I knew for a fact that was not the entirety of the sex life that God wanted me to live (or that I wanted me to live for that matter). But...how do my God knowledge and spirit walk relate to my sex life? The two were more closely related than one would think. You see, my moral compass and societal expectations of what women "should" and "shouldn't" be or do, played a huge role in how I processed the sexual thoughts and experiences I was and wasn't having. After taking some very deliberate and intentional steps, I was able to discover and address some key factors that prevented me from experiencing my personal goals and I'm here to share my "Journey to Ecstasy" with you. I went from having no orgasms at all to being a multi-orgasmic woman through a series of steps that started with mere conversation. So yea...it's fitting that I wrote a book to invite others into the very first step of that journey, let's talk about it!

Everyone loves a fruitful conversation. You know...the kind that raises an eyebrow, engages your very soul and gets you thinking long after it's over. Well, this book is definitely a facilitator of that kind of dialogue. It's divided into 3 distinct sections (parts). The first part details the concept of why we don't talk about sex, the second suggests reasons why we should talk about sex more, and the final section explores the possibilities that can come about as a result of said conversations.

Throughout the book there are several questions that organically come about. I encourage you to actually pause and answer these questions. Don't just gloss over or keep reading for reading's sake, set aside a moment and truly engage in order to get the most out of this book and reading experience. You may even want to take notes as you deliberately dive into your current mindset towards sex and how that impacts your life and perspective.

I love talking and connecting with people, it's truly one of my favorite pastimes. I pride myself on being a "straight-shooter" and I don't mind getting to the point (no matter the subject). I get a secret thrill out of saying the thing that everyone is thinking, but no one is willing to say and I'm not easily embarrassed. Honestly, I consider it a gift. I don't remember the exact moment, but one day I became ultra-aware of just how silent I was about sex and sex-related topics, but I do know I couldn't rationalize it...even to myself. I had some questions, and my natural inclination was not to ask but to leave them unanswered. I needed answers! I wanted to talk! I decided to push past my mental framework, I didn't know who I should go to with those thoughts and ideas but I knew I had to go to someone. I had to first start with me!

So, how do I stir up the conversation? The conversation that will ultimately revolutionize my sex life. Do I talk to a doctor? No, these weren't really medical topics, so to speak. Do I go to friends? I could, but there's a reason why we hadn't "gone there before", so--how would that work at this moment? I could and did talk to my husband, but he doesn't have a vagina, so his perspective would be limited so to speak. While he could engage in fruitful conversation, his input would be somewhat restricted as opposed to the perspective of someone with a similar lived experience or body type. I knew I had to do something more; I just didn't know what. I had to dive into some very poignant truths for myself so I could be able to reach out to others. I decided to set out on a mission to strike up conversations about sex with 100 different women; thus, the journey of this book was born.

It's no secret that women stand to gain far more than we stand to lose when we intentionally unite, uplift, and encourage each other. I'm a living witness of this! Of course, we can harm each other in unimaginable ways as well, but that's not why we're here, and that doesn't negate the worth of our connection and ability to help one another. There is fullness available in conversation for the up-and-coming generations and those before us. In the ways that iron can sharpen iron, we can use our perspectives to strengthen one another directly. Plainly put, we need to talk about sex more! Both in communities of faith and the world at large. We need to increase our discussion about the things that *truly* matter to us in general. This book serves as a facilitator to just one of the topics that tend to be "tucked away" from the spotlight while being "front and center stage" at the same time: SEX.

Like any other practice, one's enjoyment and expertise stand to improve with time and repetition. I have seen and experienced firsthand the benefits of talking transparently about sex with the women in my immediate proximity. The more I talked, the more I found myself empowered. I've shared my personal story and listened to women who were willing to share theirs. I've resonated with some experiences and also dove into research to find answers and solutions to situations influencing some of my sisters' journeys. Honey, this thing can get complicated, but I want you to know and remember "there's nothing new under the sun". From delicate topics like sexual abuse all the way to erotic wonders like orgasms intentionally brought about with mere thought, all of it is on the table! We're in this together, and I've made it my mission to make sure we do this well!

There was a time when my perspective toward sex was shrouded by negative connotations, which unknowingly prohibited the ecstasy that belonged to me. Thankfully, this is no longer my story. I had invisible boundaries and constraints not built on faith or love but stereotypes and shame. Amongst other things, deliberately seeking out conversations about sex continue to dissolve the very barriers that restricted my soul-shaking sex potential, and I want to share this voyage with you.

I'm here to talk about sex with women who have been told both directly and indirectly that it's somehow inappropriate or unbecoming to do so. Can you think of the countless ways that the restriction of conversations about sex has impacted lives, families and communities? It's tragic! Sex is a beautiful activity of passion and expression, and whether you choose to take part in it or not, the very conversation about it should not be restricted as much as it is. This book will dive into the *Complexities of Ecstasy*; I hope you can swim!

PART I: WE DON'T TALK ABOUT SEX ENOUGH!

CHAPTER 1: PENETRATING SILENCE

 Listen to the silence, it has so much to say."

— RUMI

I get it. Sex is an extremely delicate and layered topic to discuss, but the fact of the matter is: sex is everywhere. Talking about sex isn't equivalent to encouraging filth, crime and uncleanliness but I feel like that's sometimes how it's treated. It's embedded in our natural human desires and passion, it's occurring in nature, and it's even manipulated in religion, popular culture, and media to seemingly irrelevant situations. Sex sells! As much as we see it, we don't directly talk about it enough. So, let's do something about it! Let's talk about sex!

The secrecy and demonization hovering over sex and conversations about it have generated a culture of unhealthy mindsets toward a very healthy and enjoyable aspect of our humanity. Why is this penetrating silence the overall norm we've somehow agreed to allow to dominate in our society, especially in communities of faith? I mean... we "talk" about it, but not in a way that dismantles stereotypes or sheds light in the darkest of places. We don't really "*talk*" about it. Conversations about sex and all of its layers in various contexts should be the norm, but that's not always the case. The truth is, there's lots of surrounding noise pulling our ears in several directions. If the noise is keeping us from truly hearing and gaining understanding, it is then equivalent to silence—penetratingly so.

WHY DON'T WE TALK ABOUT IT?

What's keeping us from discussing it? Well, there are countless contributors to this cause. There's fear associated with others' perception of you based on what you've shared. Will they judge me? Will I have control over the conclusions that people draw as a result of the information I share? Is it worth it? These are just a few questions that we may sometimes have. Additionally, how will the information I share impact my partners' feelings and people's presumptions about them? There's also the idea that the topics discussed directly relate to a person's experiences, and that's not necessarily the case. Sometimes, we just want to talk. The uncertainty of the answers to those questions is more than enough to keep one's lips sealed and encourage them to navigate sex-related topics on their own or not at all.

I remember discussing my desire to write this book with one of my relatives. One of the things that stood out to me was just how ignorant I was to a lot of things. I mean, I knew I had a lot of learning to do, but after the conversation, I felt like a foreigner in a distant land. Her experience and depth of knowledge up to that point were *starkly* different from mine. My little "hang-ups and boundaries" seemed to have never crossed her mind. We were both equally impressed with each other's story, thinking, "You *really* think like that?" Her awareness and candor were truly something to behold. Frankly, a lot of the information she shared could only come through experiences—experiences that I didn't have and hadn't planned on having either...and that's ok. Talking about them at least gave me the opportunity to examine my own thoughts, feelings, and biases. I made the decision to note and be inspired by her transparency instead of scrapping the idea of writing this book due to all the information I clearly didn't know because I knew that it would help countless others.

TABOO AS IT GETS

I didn't realize just how oddly hushed we all were concerning talks about sex until I was practically an adult. Prior to that point, the muted nature of the "taboo" conversational topic was an acceptable norm to me and apparently those around me as well. Before you even try to claim the idea that we do "talk" about sex enough or even formulate the argument that we talk about it too much, just take a moment to consider if you think most people would truly agree. I understand that many people don't have a problem talking about sex and sex-related topics, but about double that amount do. If you have no problem talking about sex and sex-related topics, then you are an exception, not the norm. Despite one's comfort or discomfort, it is vital that we all share in the responsibility of understanding why the topic is taboo and the effect that has on society at large. In spite of the differences in our experiences, upbringing, and personal opinions and beliefs, we *all* are stakeholders of this essential conversation for the safety, pleasure, and well-being of humanity in general.

CONVERSATION IN MODERATION

Now don't get me wrong, I'm not advocating for everyone to run up and down the street screaming out "orgasms, clits, and scrotums!", but I am advocating for us not to cringe as much or shy away when we hear those words. We are so used to the routine of not conversing about sex that the mere mention of terms associated with our anatomy brings about feelings of embarrassment or shame.

CODENAMES

There is a lot of creativity invested in not saying certain words, but what if we applied that same effort and energy toward engaging in meaningful conversations about sex? How much do you think it would alter the current taboo nature of the conversation? I dare to say it would contribute greatly to dismantling the negative connotations and structures of control that currently exist.

The discomfort associated with talking about sex and sex-related topics has caused us to create a plethora of codenames, both universal and unique, that people use as a cop-out to prevent us from even saying words to describe our basic anatomy.

Why do certain words make people so uncomfortable?

In a world full of "wee-wee's," "coo-coo's," and "bum-bum's," we should find it just as easy to use the anatomically accurate terms ... after all, they both refer to the same parts. Say it with me, "PENIS, VAGINA, ANUS," and there are several more.

Why are these words viewed in such a different light?

Even if someone isn't uncomfortable using the terms, it's often found that he or she will still use the codenames or restrict him/herself from using the accurate terms because it's simply the norm or to make others more comfortable. If we implement language referring to our anatomical parts that sounds more "appropriate," we can almost pretend like we're not actually talking about those parts. We even rename them pleasant and unrelated things in effort to put a positive spin on them, but therein lies the problem. While there's nothing wrong with nicknames, I have yet to hear of one for a chin or elbow. Furthermore, we don't need to put a positive spin on something that isn't negative to begin with, right?

The secrecy and demonization of sex talk has generated a culture of unhealthy mindsets toward conversations about a very healthy and enjoyable aspect of our very humanity. Sure, people may have side conversations with people they trust, or perhaps someone had the "birds and the bees" talk, but why is that the norm?

Why is this deafening silence concerning conversations about sex the overall norm we've agreed to in society?

THE EVOLUTION OF LANGUAGE

There are several cultural and generational words that evolve over time. It's gotten to the point where even though it was already a taboo conversation to have, it graduates uniquely with each passing period.

> In Genesis 4:1 the bible says Adam "knew" his wife and she conceived... He *"knew"* her alright!

Nowadays, people aren't necessarily using the words "know" or "knew" to refer to sex. Beyond the ever so popular "mating," "intercourse," and "lovemaking," we have some very vivid and interesting words that commonly replace sex.

Challenge: How many synonyms for the word "sex" can you think of? Which of them do you prefer to use, and in what context? Why?

Your choice of words can be extremely telling of your comfort in conducting or participating in conversations about sex, **so what is your word choice telling you?**

WHAT'S THE HOLD-UP?

Sex isn't the only taboo conversation out there. Another major one I can think of off the top of my head is personal finance. It's easier to speak of averages or ideal situations, but the bottom line is that money conversations are very personal as well. Sometimes people consider it extremely rude and inappropriate to discuss finances or ask certain questions. Growing up, I wasn't really "aware" of my parents' salaries or financial dealings. Not only did I not know, but

the thought never really crossed my mind enough to ask—
very similar to certain topics related to sex. I just didn't
know what I didn't know. It wasn't until I got my first
salaried position as a Kindergarten teacher that my father
and I had a passing conversation about it. I was excited to
get my first "real" job; I couldn't wait to call my parents to go
over the details of my contract.

Now, even though up to that point, we hadn't really
discussed how much I wanted or expected to make, I just
felt like they "deserved" to know. They had been taking care
of me for my entire life, and for the first time, I would be
able to take care of myself. We were breaking up financially
in a sense, and I was eager to finally be independent. Like a
newborn doe, I was ecstatic to stand on my own feet and
"figure things out" no matter how inexperienced I was. My
father and I talked about several aspects of my finances, and
that conversation was very illuminating. In response to my
presentation, he reminisced on his starting salary compared
to that of his retirement. Oddly, this transparency made me
feel somewhat closer to my father. I really felt like we were
having an "adult" conversation.

As I reflect on my life, I'm 100% certain that if I had known
certain things, I would've definitely made more informed
choices. The conversation with my father brought about a
different level of access to him. A simple statement of
disclosure somehow brought us closer together. In terms of
conversations about sex, those moments of disclosure are
even more strained. But why? Now wait: before we move
forward, I'm not saying I or anyone else should share details
of our sex lives with our fathers. While the conversations
would be awkwardly hilarious, I respect the fact that we
have other things to talk about. However, I am advocating

for us to engage in meaningful conversations with the people who are closest to us as much as possible. I mention this story because from that moment forward I began to analyze things differently. I had access to a lot of the financial decisions my father made prior to that point and in an instant I gained much deeper context. Imagine the impact that forthright conversations about sex can have in your immediate community and the world at large.

A lot of times, we withhold information or shy away from "taboo" topics with the very people that mean the most to us with virtuous intentions in mind. We don't want our own decisions to have a negative impact on others. We don't want to shame others if our experiences are vastly different. We don't want to get into a debate or argument because of opposing views. We essentially want to leave the canvas blank and let the individual live out his or her own journey or start from scratch. There's an underlying thread of mystery and reservation, and it's not all bad, but the resulting pact of silence produces invisible lines that divide us and ultimately restrict our collective growth.

Conversations about sex and sex-related topics are not just about "recreation and reproduction" but are essential to mental health and advocacy as well. Familiarizing ourselves with the topic as much as possible is an opportunity to liberate and evaluate the plain as it stands. For instance, sex trafficking is at an all-time high! That's no secret, and the numbers continue to sky-rocket at an alarming rate. According to several different sources, there are millions of people trafficked daily and exploited for the profit and sexual pleasure of their capturers. Statistics and true data concerning the actual number of people trafficked is enveloped within the numbers of missing persons and undocumented disappearances. Frankly put, we don't actually know just how many people have been trafficked. In terms of protecting people from it and educating those affected by it, society at large should be far more equipped than we currently are. Furthermore, in the fortunate event that one is returned home from being trafficked, we as a collective community should have far more restorative language available than solely that of pity and horror.

As I type, I think about my own children, Joy and Jada. Although they are but a toddler and infant now, I think about how my husband and I plan to discuss taboo topics with them. My toddler who will proudly announce that "Mommy's booboo stinks in the potty" to a random store clerk, or yell "what's that smell?" when someone's hygiene is a bit compromising, holds back nothing. I can only imagine her broadcasting my business on the mountain top. "My mommy is multi-orgasmic" or "sex is a great stress relief exercise". I'm not trying to explain that stuff to her future teachers, but I might as well get ready. So, I get it, there must be wisdom and boundaries applied, but neither wisdom nor boundaries are an excuse to refuse to navigate these topics of conversation altogether. We are obligated to first grant ourselves permission to navigate difficult conversations before we can make ourselves available to converse with others.

MEDIA INFLUENCE: CENSORSHIP

Television censorship has a lot to do with how we tend to discuss sex or categorize what's "appropriate" to visualize on the big screen. It wasn't until the 1940's or so that couples could be aired sharing the same bed. Prior to that, bedrooms were either avoided or depicted with two separate beds on television broadcasts. This is significant because this marks a distinct moment in media history where marriage and relationships were depicted differently from sex and pleasure. The first "gentleman's magazine" *Playboy* was published in the 50's, and it contained sexy images of women—unlike the "neat," "gowned" wives who barely made the cut for TV. The difference between these two images stamped a significant message to viewers concerning the suggested roles and behaviors of women. The message was essentially this: wives should be depicted differently than sex symbols. If women were encouraged to be "ladies" or groomed to be "wives," then there was a subconscious lesson that they should avoid being "sexy" or that "sexiness" is preserved for mens visual pleasure as opposed to a state of being or feeling a woman can access.

In the church and religious circles, a disproportionate amount of responsibility has been placed on women to be "decent" or "modest" instead of men to exhibit self-control and respect. Don't get me wrong, there's room in conversation and lifestyle for both, but because of this disparity, women often find themselves gridlocked into secrecy and shame in situations where they shouldn't be, competing in a battle strategically designed for them to lose.

We're surrounded by sex and messages about sex in practically every area of our lives, yet we don't have the appropriate platforms to directly discuss it, nor do we even expect to be able to. From the big screen to commercials and advertisements, *sex sells*! Look around. Direct and indirect conversations about sex should be commonplace and full of transparency and *truth,* but the most common conversations we experience are often indirect!

Can you recall your last conversation about sex? Was it direct or indirect?

The most popular message about sex from many church communities is simply, "Don't do it unless you're married," followed by the ever so popular, "The marriage bed is undefiled." There is so much to discuss before, during, and even after marriage! To get to these conversations, we must first directly address the walls built up around them. I mean think about it, I'm not a millionaire yet...but there's no restriction on discussing or researching money or best financial practices. Conversations about sex and the very act aren't necessarily synonymous, so let me ask you this:

Do you have any walls restricting your mindset or conversations? If so, why are these walls there and how do they serve or restrict you?

ACCESSIBILITY TO SEX CONTENT

When I was a child, I remember couples "kissing" or fondling on TV, but sex was very much insinuated and not nearly as visual as it is on television today. Children in this generation are growing up in a day and age where sex content is no longer as much of a "secret" as it used to be. The accessibility and popularization of the internet brings all manner of things to our fingertips. Gone are the days of guessing.

I realized just how much access we have to information when my family and I went to visit a family near and dear to our hearts one afternoon. They had just welcomed a new baby boy to their fold. Our friends' four-year-old son asked his mother if we could take a walk to the nearby park. It was a fairly nice day, but we didn't know if it was going to rain or be too cool for the baby or anything. His mother replied, "Well, if we do end up going to the park, it would depend on the weather."

Before she could get the words out of her mouth, the boy squeals out in the cutest little four-year-old lisp, "Awexa, what is the wedder today?"

Instantly, Alexa replied, "The weather today is 79 degrees and sunny."

A smile crept across his little face as he made eye contact with his mother. It was in that moment that I realized that information is even more readily available than it's ever been. In generations past, you had to actually spell the words out or at least sound them out to type them into a search engine. Before that, there were movies and magazines. Before that, I'm guessing you would have to look in an encyclopedia or something ... I don't know. The point is, it takes little to no effort these days to be drawn into a conversation about sex, and we have the unique opportunity to dictate how to steer this ship now and for generations to come.

Our bodies are some intricately designed units, and that's no secret. Yet the conversations are limited because society has a general idea of what's "normal." No one wants to be labeled "different" with a negative connotation and be reduced to that alone. No one wants to become "odd" or "abnormal." So, I get it; we don't talk about certain things. However, there is so much life in a testimony. We sit up and ruminate over certain topics and ideas that feel rare, but these ideas may not actually be as unique as we think. There's nothing new under the sun.

Our experiences are so rich in value and can save lives simply by letting someone else know, "You are not alone." Can you imagine how differently some of your life's situations would've played out if you had access to someone with an identical or similar story that was willing to share the nitty gritty details?

SELF-TALK

Before we can talk to anyone about anything, we must be willing to explore our own personal thoughts, beliefs, biases, and experiences.

What are your personal philosophies about sex, and where did they come from?

While some questions may be easy to answer and expound upon, others may require a bit of thought and pause. These moments are empowering to preserve the values we hold dear and also addressing ideas that don't serve or actually cause us harm.

I don't remember how old I was, but I remember as a very young child hearing insults between older kids and some adults in movies and stuff. One of the biggest insults I had ever heard was someone saying, "Suck my dick". I clutched my pearls typing that, but I had to write it. For the life of me, I couldn't conceptualize someone actually doing it, and the gall of a person even saying that took my breath away. You see, I didn't know that oral sex was actually "a thing" prior to that point. So for years it just seemed like a mean insult people would sling. I equated it to like "you eat booboo" or something like that. It just seemed gross to me to put a mans sexual organ in your mouth. After some time, I began to hear rumors about people actually intentionally doing it and again my innocence led the way for my ignorance, I thought people were just trying to be hurtful. As a young girl, I didn't know much but I knew I didn't plan on putting my mouth on someone's urine organ...well, some things change over time.

Can you think of any thoughts or ideas you had when you were younger that you no longer have?

One of the reasons we don't talk about certain things is that sometimes we don't realize there is anything to discuss. Carrying the weight of yesterday, what we're taught and what we assume, we often allow ourselves to be subjected to ideas that aren't even our own. Of all the conversations we choose not to have, the most important ones are the ones we have with ourselves. Nobody can make you discuss a topic or engage in a conversation that you don't want to have; however, that is no excuse for not having the conversations yourself. Free your mind to entertain thoughts, ideas, and possibilities centered around sex and sex-related topics in order to rationalize your thoughts, feelings and beliefs.

CHAPTER 2: FAUXGASMS AND SUCH...

 You can't wake a person that's pretending to be asleep"

— NAVAJO PROVERB

W omen have been "faking it" since the beginning of time. From imposter syndrome to flat-out lying intentionally. People are really out here faking all kinds of things, including but not limited to orgasms. We fake satisfaction, we fake contentment, we even fake peace of mind. I'm saying "we" because I feel it's necessary to include myself in this conversation. Even if you aren't faking all of the things listed, you for darn sure can relate to not being fully transparent in one way or another. In relation to sex, a lot of people regularly perform fauxgasms (fake orgasms) with a series of moans, gestures, and Oscar-worthy talent performances.

Have you ever had a "fauxgasm" or pretended to be satisfied

when you actually weren't? What was your primary reason for doing so?

Contentment, happiness, even personal fulfillment in life are often feigned because we feel like it's the "right" thing to do to maintain the image we have worked so hard to design. Some people are so good at faking they don't even recognize they're doing it.

I can recall times that I flashed the brightest smile all the way to the security of my car where I could safely bawl my eyes out, or times where I would compliment someone on something that I actually thought was atrocious. Lord, forgive me! There were times when I answered the question "How are you?" with an automatic "Fine, and you?" when I was far from fine and was fully aware of it. All FAKE!!! FAKE FAKE FAKE! Because of this fake reality we often live in, conversations about sex are heavily restricted for the majority. Now don't go out and, with brutal honesty, tear down the walls of everything that was ever built. However, I do want to challenge us to take a moment and examine the areas of our lives where we are faking it and ask ourselves why.

What is the most common thing that people "fake" contentment about in society, and why? What are the consequences of faking it? What areas of life do you feel the need to fake it, and why? What adjustments can you make to address the areas in which you haven't been as truthful as possible?

Concerning sex, women have been known to "fake it" in large part to stroke their partners' egos, convince their partners that they are enjoying themselves, and prevent further conversation about the absence of the anticipated response. Some women simply don't know what else to do. The other part is to replace the lie with some "other truth"... or truths.

In a way, we have formed a societal norm to appear complacent, even if that's the furthest thing from the truth. Then, we normalize the false narrative by calling people who share their imperfections "weak" or "complainers." We even go as far as to challenge their ability to conduct themselves in society. People are actually punished for not suffering in silence—this explains why it is often difficult to reach out for help. The fact of the matter is, it's become the norm to "fake it"—whatever "it" is, but faking it takes work! To be truthful and vulnerable is actually considered rare and can even be considered rude or inappropriate at times, but it is truly the only way to break out of the brainwashing of society as it pertains to the topic at hand and realize God's best for all of our lives. So take a stand! Take hold of the power you've sacrificed by not being truthful, against such there is no crime. You don't have to hop on stage and tell all of your business, but you can make an internal decision not to live a life full of lies.

The sound, the look, and the posture can all be authentic indicators of pleasure; likewise, they can also be feigned and manipulated rather well. Sure, these things are strong components of the visual and physical act of sex, but there is a strong disparity between mastering these acts for performance sake versus personal pleasure. In the world of unofficial rumors and official sexual studies, it's no secret that men on average orgasm more than women. Here are some startling statistics according to Psychology Today[1]:

*"A comprehensive analysis of 33 studies over 80 years
found that during vaginal intercourse, just 25 percent
of women consistently experience an orgasm, about half
of women sometimes have an orgasm, 20 percent seldom
or ever have orgasms, and about 5 percent never have
orgasms."*

I'm not going to lie, learning that only about a quarter of
sexually active women orgasm regularly made my heart
ache in a way I can't quite explain (and I'm not going to even
try to guess how these numbers would change if we
exclusively surveyed a pool of women in the church and
communities of faith). I mean, it makes sense seeing as to
how we don't talk about sex in general but—*wow*! Everyone
knows someone who will broadcast great sex tales, but
where are the people sharing the other side of the coin?
Where are the bad sex stories? Where are the "I suck at sex"
stories or the "My partner sucks at sex" stories? These are
not the most commonly broadcasted stories because...who
wants to own that narrative without the security of knowing
it won't cause additional harm. People would rather deal
with the consequences of not being fully transparent to
reduce the risk of appearing ignorant or deficient in some
way. This not only applies to matters of sex, but all the other
categories of faking, too! If you weren't yet convinced of the
necessity of these conversations centered around sex before,
I hope you're convinced now!

TRANSPARENCY CHECK

Is your sex life perfect? I know that's a broad question but
answer truthfully. Of course not! If it is, then you need to

take a moment and evaluate what convinces you that things couldn't be even better. Regardless of where you stand, it's important to conduct honest reflection and mental inventory concerning your mindset and sex perspective. In your immediate circle, what is the culture around conversations about sex?

What is the nature of your girlfriend check-ins? Do you talk to your closest friends about sex? Why or why not? Would the women closest to you feel comfortable talking to you about sex and sex related experiences?

Without embarrassing yourself or disclosing more than you are willing, there are ways to ask questions and get answers.

Sex is an ever-evolving and developing topic, as it should be. Naturally, our bodies change over time. My thirteen-year-old body is not the same as my 32-year-old, post-two-baby body. Not better or worse, just different. Likewise, my 56-year-old body will yet again prove herself with another layer of sophistication, I'm sure. As one's body and mindset evolve, it is essential to continuously grow and learn so that both body and mind can collaborate to create the healthiest you possible.

GETTING READY

Society takes certain cues from the media about how women are expected to look and behave. Women are expected to wear bras, spanks, and undergarments to keep "things" in place, in addition to sporting natural-looking yet evident makeup enhancements to our faces. Makeup is so common that in many circles, normal faces are considered unprofessional and can even signify a lack of care. Hairstyles, lashes, eyebrows, mani/pedis, jewelry, and fragrance are all in the box of "getting ready." And these are just the ending products, don't get me started on the pre-work: skincare routines, anti-aging rituals, and time itself just to name a few.

If this doctored image is the one that a woman puts most of her effort into, who is the one engaging in sex? While sex is, for the most part, a physical act for men, it is a very mental one for women. Let me be clear; I'm not insinuating that women who are dolled up aren't having great sex or conversations about it. I am saying that appearance doesn't have as much to do with the sexual mindset of that woman as one would think. When setting out to write this book, I made the goal to interview as many women as I could about sex and the conversations they have/had about it. I was somewhat shocked to find that appearance efforts and quality of experience weren't always parallel. What I mean is that the women who seem to meet and exceed society's and the media's beauty standards would share experiences that were sometimes lackluster; meanwhile, the women who didn't seem as interested in perfecting the media's perception of their appearance were illuminating some of the most eye-opening information and experiences.

SEX DRIVE AND MENTAL LOAD

Part of the issue that women can face that competes with our sexual pleasure is the mental load of daily responsibilities. The average man has a sex drive that is vastly different from the average woman. This doesn't mean that women don't want sex; it just means that men tend to want it much more! In addition to that, society's patriarchal structure tends to support a man's sex life and habits more so than it does the average woman's. There are several factors that influence one's sex drive; it's not like it just falls from the sky. I heard about this concept describing the "mental load" people carry, and it illuminated so much to me, especially concerning sex and conversations related to it. In the patriarchal structure of our society, most often women tend to act as the "manager" of the home. Restocking supplies (groceries shopping), custodial duties (cleaning), culinary arts (cooking), and a host of other responsibilities—while being expected in many cases to maintain a full-time job outside of the home. It can be extremely exhausting and seem impossible to do it all well, but some tend to figure it out! Men, on the other hand, are most often responsible for their job outside of the home and are expected to "help" with the tasks of the household from time to time. If the aforementioned household tasks are managed by a man it is considered impressive or praise-worthy. I know this isn't always the case, but it does happen in many households. The woman is then forced to manage both home and work with working mental systems to make life easier for her and those around her. In addition to that, she may multitask, doing laundry while dinner is cooking, and helping the kids do their homework. When something goes awry, the people around her may make the remark, "You should've asked for help!" as though the tasks she's juggling are exclusively her responsibility or solely for her benefit. The expectation that the work she does that benefits everyone around her is her responsibility, and the job of also delegating tasks is all a part of the mental load she carries.

Time is of the essence, and this sometimes can dampen the "mood." Managing system after system is second nature at times, but every now and then, a woman will be made aware of the weight of her mental load and this is where the conflict starts to brew. She may be staring at her counterpart, who equally benefits, but is blissfully unaware of all of the mental effort that goes into sustaining life as they know it. Or she may be tempted by the idea of being served or being on vacation and being rescued from her day to day responsibilities. Now throw in that pot the fact that she may not be one of the twenty-something percent having regular orgasms. Whew girl! While sex is great, sometimes it gets pushed a little further down on the priority list because there are some other tasks that demand immediate attention and mental effort. Adversely, sometimes sex is prioritized over other responsibilities to even make the daily mundane tasks doable.

How does your mental load impact your sex drive? Are your sex drive and sex life parallel? If you're not sexually active, what factors can you think of that may impact one's sex life or sex drive? What adjustments can you make to your current mental load to compliment or enhance your sex life?

So what's a girl to do? If you're wondering how to managing your mental load and mindset toward sex, consider what things are on your plate and why. Survey your daily schedule:

What day to day demands take up most of your time?

Once you do that, take a moment to consider if you didn't do those things how your life could change. If you want a better mindset toward sex, chances are you need to make room for it. You need to shift some of the thoughts, ideas and tasks that currently occupy the space you want to free. I remember my first year of marriage when my husband and I decided to move to "The Big Apple". Our quaint little apartment wasn't equipped with a washer and dryer, which meant that we would have to go to the laundromat or have a service pick up our clothes and do them for us. I couldn't fathom the idea of someone washing my dirty panties so my husband agreed to take on the entirety of the laundry duties. Laundry became an obstacle in my mental path, so we moved it. While he was at the laundromat, I could start dinner or tend to some other household task I wanted to complete. Making that adjustment freed me up to do other things, it was a minor adjustment, but it changed my life. As a "newly wed" I learned really quickly that traditional gender roles didn't have to apply. My husband was willing...I didn't have to turn him down because I felt like it was a "womans role" to do certain things.

In what ways you can adjust your current way of life to lighten your mental load?

THE DIFFERENCE BETWEEN MEN AND WOMEN

While men on average seem to hit their sexual peak around age 22, women don't hit theirs until they're about 42. There is a 20-year disparity here. This makes sense because men most often experience their first orgasms at a younger age than women typically do. We tend to culture young boys to experience sexual freedom and liberation a lot more than girls both inside and outside of the church. While talks of "wet dreams," indulging in imagination and masturbation, is more common when addressing young boys, the opposite equivalent is practically absent for young girls. A study performed by Alfred Kinsey in 1950 revealed that "95% of men had experienced an orgasm by the time they were in their late teens, compared to just 20% of women of the same age."[2] Now, this is the perfect scenario for a cougar and a cub, but it can be a little less than ideal for pairs outside of that description. I say this because differences in sex drive is a lot of times a source of contention within many adult relationships.

> A cougar is described as an older woman seeking the sexual and romantic attention of a younger man (in many cases young enough to be her son).

While on average, men crave sex the most in their early 20s, the life and sex drive of a woman in her early 20s is full of many barriers that can potentially hinder her from truly indulging in her own psychological sexual voyage. This disparity can be caused by mental load, ignorance, lack of educational resources, insecurities, self-consciousness, negative stigmas, religion, fear, misinformation, discomfort, the list goes on and on. By age 40, a lot of the barriers loosen as a newer level of transparency, and self-awareness emerges. Thus, women tend to hit their sexual peaks a bit later in life.

BRAINWASHED

Society has been brainwashed to perform as "expected," and the priority of truth and honesty gets lost somewhere between the center of our souls and deepest desires along the way. We smile on the outside when we're practically dying internally. Think about events in popular culture with well-known public figures and how shocking it is to learn of their "humanity" by way of the exposure of their mistakes or weaknesses. We intentionally dress ourselves up for events and functions while leaving our hearts and minds heavy-burdened with the cares of life.

MIRROR, MIRROR ON THE WALL

How you perceive yourself informs your instincts and behaviors, but more often than not people see more than the attributes you intend to display.

If you hold a mirror up to your soul, what things would truly be reflected?

Let me go ahead and tell you: you'd see the truth—it would leak out! The unadulterated raw truth of who you are and what lies within is the loudest part of the "real" you. Your assets won't be there, your looks won't be there, the things in this physical world you've worked so hard to secure simply will not be there. The real you will be staring back at you—**does your effort-created persona match the "you" staring back?**

> 1 Samuel 16:7 ... for man looketh on the outward appearance, but the LORD looketh on the heart.

The true you is the part of you who needs to be able to speak on your behalf. This is the part of you who has access to the fruit of the spirit and true happiness. So why is It that people are conditioned to speak on the surface when we know good and well there isn't much going on up there anyway? Conversations about sex and the impact it has on our lives, occur way down deep in the depths of one's true nature, intentions, and mental liberty. Your sex life can only be truly revolutionized from this place.

CHAPTER 3: AS SEEN ON TV...

Porn and Performance

 The problem with pornography is that it does not reveal too much of a woman but too little."

— POPE JOHN PAUL II

From shameless consumers in the open to pastors and leaders in secret, porn is a lot more common in people's personal lives than many would publicly admit. In the age of social media and plentiful internet accessibility, pornographic imagery is available at every turn. In generations past, one would perhaps have to work a little harder to find certain images. They may have to get their hands on a magazine/book or wait for a late-night or premium channel movie. Perhaps they would be able to get their hands on a VHS to watch a triple X film, or a "flick" as it's sometimes referred to. I remember hearing male friends joking about how they used to circulate floppy discs amongst their friend circles in elementary school with short pornographic clips on them in school. Though the clips were only about 20 seconds at most, it probably would take about 20 minutes just for the videos to download with dial-up internet and outdated desktop computers. Today, you don't even have to download anything. Porn is steadily being produced and sought after.

What is/or has been your experience with porn? What kind of influence did or does it have on you? What kind of influence do you think it has on men versus the influence it has on women and why? What influence has it had on society at large? What influence has is had on the church and communities of faith?

SEARCH ENGINES

Some of the first internet search engines were made public in the early '90s. The ability to research practically anything immediately got easier when we gained access to simply type a keyword or phrase and allow the encrypted algorithms to do all of the hard work. This was a game-changer for many as the ability to "privately" seek out porn became more accessible. They could just search for the images they craved on the internet. Sometimes you could stumble across sexual images accidentally if a word or phrase could be interpreted as a sexual connotation. I remember in third grade my computer teacher had our class research our future careers. Yikes! Naughty nurses and sexy cheerleaders flooded our screens. Without parental controls our access was seemingly limitless. We pulled up all kinds of images, and called her over to our computer every time. She was mortified! I'm not going to lie, at some point it became a game to feign innocence and watch her try to save our eye gates.

Gone are the days of merely imagining or dreaming; one can conjure up whatever image they desire within an instant and materialize it for their viewing pleasure. Due to this recent and evolving accessibility to imagery, fantasy, and erotica, we are in a place where we have to make certain topics of conversation commonplace in order to maintain and normalize a standard—especially in the church! Brace yourself, with or without your approval, children can and will see sexual images. Lifewise they will, in their humanity, feel sexual feelings. These things shouldn't be silenced or masked as if they don't exist.

Not only is porn highly accessible, it is also highly informative. Beyond that, I'd dare to say it serves as one of the primary teachers of sex education. If one doesn't gain information from it directly, he or she interacts with it or is taught by others who have.

How old were you when you became aware of the existence of porn? Do you think you were mature enough to be presented with the information?

Porn is a very loud and demanding teacher! You don't have to agree or fully understand it for it to impact you. You're going to pay attention! With lighting, cameras, casts and crew, the scenes are shot with exaggerated assistance, and it is visually appealing. According to research by the NSPCC, of the adolescents who had been exposed to porn, 28% were first exposed by accident, 19% were unexpectedly shown pornography by someone else, and only 19% searched for it intentionally. (NSPCC, 2016).[1] The majority of children that encounter porn for the first time do so without their own intent or effort. Sit with that for a minute! While some people are repulsed (or pretend to be repulsed) by the objective and lustful nature of the industry, that hasn't stopped it from becoming the empire it essentially is.

There is a multi billion-dollar demand for porn, and it successfully maintains this multi-billion dollar industry by appealing to visual desires, fantasies, and lusts. Naturally, those billions are upheld by sexual enhancement drugs, multiple scenes, varying angles, and production arrangements that aim to elicit and manipulate certain responses from the viewer. This is a research-based industry that is continuously evolving. Let's be clear, I'm not advertising for porn, but trust me, with or without my mention, porn isn't going anywhere! We might as well talk about it. Things are not always as they seem, of course, but the reality is that the average consumer doesn't seem to mind. We are cultivated to indulge in fantasy and curated images. As young as infancy, we display cartoons and characters to children. They are groomed in the idea that things don't have to be realistic or believable in order for us to enjoy them. The problem occurs when people don't develop the boundaries or critical thinking skills to discern the differences, crossing or confusing the expectations and production of porn with real life.

ADDICTED

One of the aspects that make pornography so successful as an industry is its addictive nature. People have to come back for more in order for the industry to survive. Simply put, it's enticing to see, and some people struggle more than others in an attempt to try to pull their eyes, money, and minds away from it. Addiction can manifest in several different forms. When I hear the term "addict," like many people, the first thought that comes to mind is that of a drug addict or alcoholic—one who has cravings beyond his/her control and suffers negative ramifications as a result , including but not limited to, self-harm. You can be addicted to darn near anything, so it's not surprising that porn and the very act of sex itself are not exempt!

The high you get from pleasurable and orgasmic adventures can send people to far distances and deep depths. Because sex is such a private act, sex addicts, like any other addict, develop mechanisms and habits that aid them in concealing their addictions. There are times when the addiction intensifies so much that the addict begins to do bizarre and egregious acts to quench their thirst because the addiction has gained more decision making power in their lives than their very will. Like drug addicts that go off looking for a stronger high, sex addicts sometimes drift off in search of the same. They familiarize themselves with their desires and various ways to induce and increase certain sensations.

Now, I'm no addiction expert, but I wanted to gain more context on addiction, so I attended a sex addicts' anonymous class. There were several people in attendance. Some people self identified as addicts, and others like me were simply present without a single word. We all sat in solidarity, humanity, and respect for the information that was being shared and all that wasn't. In addition to details of promiscuity, STDs, and severe lapses in judgment, the people present also seemed to share a similar sound of remorse—shame even. They shared their experiences with details that made me clutch my pearls until my fingers went numb. I don't know who I thought was going to be there...criminals, pedophiles, and perverts I guess. I mean,

I'm sure they were certainly in attendance as well, but I wasn't expecting the "average" folk. It was the grandpa who shared his story that opened my eyes differently. I could hear the years in the cracks of his voice. This man had been married for decades, and his sexual addiction makes it hard for him to sustain a normal life. He had spent a lot of his money on prostitutes and his time in sketchy places in hopes of fulfilling his sexual fantasies almost daily. Can you imagine living your senior years married to someone that has drained hundreds and thousands of dollars that the both of you planned to retire with? Some days were better than others, and he spoke well of those days and described them as "victories." However, the costs as he described them made us all shiver. Having unfettered access to money and time is the perfect breeding ground for addiction, and even without those two an addict can and will find a way. Addiction is much bigger than mere "poor choices", it's a chemical shift in the brain that requires unique attention and creative navigation. Conversations about addiction are delicate and must be met with wisdom and discernment.

So ok, now we know our neighbors, community service workers, family members, teachers, pastors/ministers—people just like you and me are the porn consumers. Porn consumption and addiction within the church is a topic within itself. Statistics can't be properly reported because a lot of people wouldn't dare self identify for fear of being tied to undesirable stigmas. Many people in the church consume and are addicted to porn because they feel that it's better to indulge with the visual medium than to actually perform the sexual task, even though indulging in the mental act is practically the same as doing it for real (Matthew 5:27). I know, I know--*it's different,* but the bigger point is that self control should be prioritized in both thought and deed. It's the very thought process that often initiates the deed. In terms of pornography consumption and addiction, people have the opportunity to familiarize themselves with experiences and imagery that they may or may not have ever had in reality.

SIDE EFFECTS

Sometimes addicts and non-addicts alike can experience sexual friction from the frequent manipulation of their genital organs that can cause damage or discomfort to their partners and/or their own bodies. I've sat through several interviews where clients described instances like calloused penis', friction burns, skin irritation, anal and vaginal tearing, nerve damage, bleeding, bruised cervixes, the list goes on and on. Porn stars sometimes leave the industry and speak out about the experiences they felt and witnessed as a result of the style and sheer quantity of sexual experiences they had or were exposed to.

Aside from the physical effects, there are also spiritual effects. Now, let me be clear, there is a distinction between frequent sex and addiction. I want to make that very clear. Over the course of time, one can have a whole lot of sex and not damage a thing nor put themselves or partner(s) in harms way. Likewise, one can have little or infrequent sex and have similar experiences. One must consider multiple factors within a storyline before making that assumption for yourself, or accusation for someone else. *So how can one determine if they are an addict or just loves sex?* The blurring or lack of boundaries may indicate a different level of yearning and potentially indicate characteristics of addiction.

An addict's body and brain function differently. It's highly likely that they would suffer from withdrawals or subject themselves to great lengths if they were to attempt to omit the source of their addiction. Some addicts become physically sick for a period of time or until their craving is satisfied. In the case of porn and sex addiction, step one is acknowledging that there is or may be an issue and to move forward from there.

ADDICTION CHECKLIST

> • Do your sexual desires have more power in your life than your own will?
> • Do you feel unable to curb your appetite or go without having sex or sexual experiences?
> • Are you ashamed or embarrassed with some of the decisions you make in order to fulfill your sexual desires?
> • Does anyone else know of the extent of your sexual cravings or activities?
> • Have you been accused of being a sex addict?
> • Are you so preoccupied with sex it becomes like a ritual to you?

Each individual has a right and opportunity to make his or her choices concerning whether or not they choose to watch porn. However, you can't watch hours upon hours of perfectly edited sex performance and masturbate until your arms go numb and expect to be uninfluenced. The choice to indulge will undoubtedly impact your thoughts and expectations. Sometimes people consume porn regularly then expect to engage in a "healthy" sexual relationship with someone and silently allow them to feel inadequate or guilty about not keeping up. There's no paycheck at the conclusion of a plain ole sex session like there is in porn, so there are boundaries that may interrupt one's fantasy ... and that's ok. I can't tell you the countless times I've heard men or boys reference something they've seen and the corresponding number of women that report not enjoying said things.

So, here's a question that is often posed.

What does God think of porn?

Before I give a direct answer, I want to paint a picture of what is happening on both sides of the screen. The actors are in a room, often with several people (lighting, directing, crew, etc.). The actors are performing the act. Then there's the audience (everybody else). I'd dare to say both the consumers and creators share significant stakes in the ordeal. There are several different layers to this. The reality is that porn is a conglomerate of things. It's difficult to say what God thinks about porn itself because it's composed of so many other factors, but we can definitively speak of those things. The bottom line is that God hates sin. If it's sinful, we can conclude he's not with it. Technology and production in biblical times was a whole lot different, and there aren't any direct scriptures on it per se. While all things are lawful, everything is not beneficial (1 Corinthians 6:12). If we begin to examine the lust, manipulation, greed, and deceit I think we arrive at a more level conversational plateau as opposed to talking about the topic in general. We can agree, those aren't God's favorites. I think a clearer way to seek God's perspective would be to ask specific questions about the layers. Exactly which part of the process are you inquiring of? Clarity of these aspects may guide you in addressing your own thoughts and feelings and better enable you to formulate your thoughts and words.

Considering the layers, each person must judge his or her own intent. Examining your own motives will lead you to the answers you seek. How does your watching porn line up with your values? Would you consent to yourself or someone you love being on the screen or performing the acts you and others seek to consume? Is there any discrepancy in what you watch and what you would do? Perhaps start there and dig deeper into your reasoning. From that investigation, like any other area of your life, pray and ask God for wisdom. My take is that everyone must examine their hearts and get to the core of their intentions and behaviors in all things.

MASTURBATION

"Scratching your own itch" is a hot topic that is yet another red zone that many people don't quite know what to say about. Long before a person reaches the age that they would intentionally masturbate for their own sexual pleasure, children and even babies naturally explore their bodies. Babies can't wait to get their diapers off to get a feel for what's going on down south. Soon thereafter, puberty comes knocking at the door. And sometimes adolescents start to "spend more time in the shower," or bottles of lotion will all of a sudden start to empty sooner than they usually would. While thinking of young boys "jacking off" by whatever means they choose is a little more normalized, we don't necessarily think about young girls doing it with as much acceptance at the same age and frequency. If we attach the messaging of a girl's worth to her "purity" or her abstaining from engaging in sexual acts period, how do we address the fact that she has natural desires and may be doing the same things? We need to be able to boldly discuss topics concerning sexuality for ourselves and the generations looking to us for guidance on how to navigate life.

So, here's the big question: *what does God think of masturbating? Is it right, is it wrong?* Similar to the question of pornography, because there are so many layers to this question, I was tempted to just leave it out altogether, but that would do a huge disservice to this book and its entire premise. I refuse to do that. So, let's rub into the layers of masturbation (pun intended) bit by bit, then return to the question. There are two primary acts at play regarding masturbating: the physical act and the mental act.

Physically, masturbation is the act of pleasuring oneself. For men, it usually looks like them stroking the shaft of their penis up and down repeatedly. However, for women it can take on several different forms, both internal and external. Internal masturbation requires something (a finger, dildo, or whatever else people stick up there) to be inserted into the vagina to elicit sexual pleasure. External masturbation requires manipulation of not only the vulva and vaginal area, but also engaging various erroneous zones. If we extend the idea of masturbation to not just the vaginal area, then this broadens our idea of self-pleasure and how we generally think about it. Breasts, nipples, thighs, and wherever else that feels good is all fair game. Then there's the mental part.

Mentally, examining masturbation is a little easier to dissect. The mental portion of masturbation is whatever thought or imaginative vehicle can get you to your destination. If said vehicle involves sin, then this is where the line can be drawn. If sin is required, we can deduce that whatever it is isn't God's best for you. If the thoughts are impure, sinful, harmful, or unhealthy, then it's safe to say those may not be the thoughts you should engage in to "get off." Our heavenly father is all for guiding us to make sound decisions, and a big part of that is intent. What are you thinking of while you get your rocks off? Pleasing yourself without having to draw up mental images contrary to your values and beliefs holds less "risk" than going for whatever images you can. I mean, if you're trying to avoid eating meat, for example, you probably shouldn't make reservations at a Brazilian steak house. In that same way, if abstinence is the goal, then you shouldn't be taking time to deliberately fantasize and engage in imaginative sex with people that you have deemed off-limits. Now, if you're thinking of your partner or not using any images at all, then the context shifts greatly. Its essential for us to consider and discuss the intricate details in order to accurately assess the heart and the behavior.

FEELING GOOD

In the beginning of my teaching career, I found myself also enrolled in cosmetology school (that season of my life is a book in and of itself). During that time, I learned so much more than the art of cosmetology and customer service. Daily, streams of people would flood the hair school, and performing services seemed to be the majority of our course load and learning experience. Naturally, I can tell stories for days about the people we encountered and experiences we had day in and day out. There is one particular experience that stands out in my mind though and I'm cringing merely thinking about it, but I'm going to go ahead and share it with you.

It was a fairly "normal" day: "normal" schedule, "normal" agenda, "normal" client stream, everything seemed quite "normal." This particular client requested a wash and roller set. "Normal", I thought. I draped her, briefly examined her hair and scalp condition, then began to rinse her hair before her shampooing service. As soon as the water touched her head, I could tell by her facial expression that she was enjoying the pleasurable sensation immensely. This wasn't starting off as "normal" as I initially thought.

After rinsing her hair, I applied some shampoo to my hand, and this is when the show began. Her breathing changed a little, then the next thing you know, she started to make a little noise and the noise became more and more pronounced. I thought to myself, "I know this woman is not sitting here moaning." It wasn't loud enough to garner my instructors attention, but it was most certainly loud enough to mortify me. Because it was cosmetology school, all services tended to be exaggerated toward "best practices" or "the right way," so there was no rushing through this service and she was loving every second of it! So here I was, *jacking this woman's head off*, and I was stuck. She was moaning and squirming, and I was just trying to do my job. I started to notice a few glances, and snickers and I tried my hardest to keep a professional mental distance. "Finish the service. Try to ignore her," I told myself, but that had to be one of the most awkward interactions I've had to date. I finished getting her off during the shampoo and made up in my mind that her conditioning was going to be cut short because she wasn't getting a second one out of me.

While that story was comical, it made me think about the fact that getting off or experiencing pleasure isn't all about the vagina; it's more about a state of mind. It's about a state of pleasurable freedom. If we look at it that way, we can remove the demonization and the idea that masturbation is *only* tied to porn and "inappropriate" images instead of enjoyment and sensual satisfaction. That woman wasn't thinking of having sex with me, or at least I hope she wasn't. I think that she was merely enjoying a massage. Now, she didn't have to moan and squirm like that publicly, but whatever. The point is, there are nerve endings and sensational areas all over our bodies, which make physical enjoyment available in various forms. The decision to explore those areas independently or with a partner depends on that person's principles and commitments.

We should be empowered to engage in thoughtful, honest, and intriguing conversations about *sex and sex related topics* —often. These conversations will shift the paradigm of toxic sex culture as we know it. These very conversations will enhance our mindsets, which can lead to better understanding and, frankly, better sex.

What aspects of masturbation do you think make it questionable for some people?

An intense scalp massage may ignite sparks of fire similar to that of a breast massage. If both acts can bring a woman to orgasm, can these acts be ranked as more or less appropriate or acceptable? Is the mere act of touching oneself the offense or the idea that it can be pleasurable? These are the some of the tucked away questions that must be brought to light in order to bring clarity to the topic thus enabling us to speak about it more transparently.

PART I: CONVERSATION CORNER

Now what:

Now that I'm more aware that we don't talk about sex enough, what should I do? Where do I go from here?

- **Never stop growing and learning!** Research, grab a book, listen to a podcast. Interrupt that silence. If you realize that you could stand a little more "sex talk" in your life, start by asking questions to yourself first. Before you speak to someone else, you have to formulate the ideas. Sometimes we possess more knowledge than we think. Think of broad ideas and concepts that you could stand to learn a little more about, then zoom in to more personal inquiries about your own life, body, and experiences.

- **Identify any areas of your life in which you've been untruthful, both consciously and subconsciously, and make a plan to address them.** What adjustments can you make to live in truth? In the age of growing social media and access to digital content, what impact has pornography and media beauty standards had on you and/or your immediate social community? Separating mental lies and truths will provide you with more clarity.

- **Find your voice.** Whether your voice is loud and booming or quiet and strained, there is a whole lifetime of development that contributes to it being what it is. Being mindful of your own voice will inform you on the next steps you need to take. Take a moment and examine how you got the voice that you have and if you want to keep it the same or make adjustments that serve you better.

GROUP SENTENCE STARTERS

Chapter 1: Penetrating Silence	Chapter 2: Fauxgasms and Such	Chapter 3: As Seen on TV
"I'm willing to talk about certain things pertaining to sex, but sometimes I don't because…"	"The raw truth is sometimes difficult to acknowledge or talk about because…"	"Because of the media's portrayal of sex and sex related content, I find myself…"

TREND BREAKERS

What would the world look like if more candid conversations about sex were held in a truthful, healthy way that actually empowered our mindsets toward sex?

Challenge: Assess the comfort level of your community. Strike up a sex-related conversation with a girlfriend or woman you trust. Here are some questions you can ask:

- How comfortable are you talking about sex (1-"I can barely say the word" to 5-"Should I be uncomfortable?")
- Have you ever faked an orgasm? Why or why not?
- What do you think is the most uncomfortable aspect of porn to discuss?

PART II: WE SHOULD TALK ABOUT SEX MORE!

CHAPTER 4: BLISSFUL IGNORANCE

 If you can't explain it simply, you don't understand it well enough"

— UNKNOWN

Ignorance is bliss, or so they say. There is a lot of information that can educate, encourage and enlighten us all when it comes to sex and conversations about it. It's necessary to talk about sex or at least allow yourself to think about it to make informed and deliberate decisions and share information with others. I cannot tell you the number of times I've witnessed the "lights come on" in someone's eyes when making a general statement about sex that they may not have experienced or heard of before. We obtain a lot of information through experience. I don't care how much experience you do or don't have, no single individual "knows it all." It behooves us to at least be able to learn and share the information we do have within our communities and inner circles. We can all benefit more through our collective knowledge and efforts.

CELIBACY AND ABSTINENCE

Some people refrain from having sex by choice, while others may do so by circumstance or some combination of the two, yet some haven't taken the time to consider the difference. Celibacy is the choice not to engage in sexual activity, often as a religious vow or commitment. Abstinence is the state of not engaging in sex outside of marriage. Masturbation may or may not be included in that definition of either, depending on who you talk to. I think it's worth mentioning that if someones personal commitment is to avoid sexual gratification in general as a lifestyle, then that commitment stands with or without a partner (if that's even truly the commitment). Further definition is required by the implementing partner to define what that means. I can't tell you the number of times that people have self identified as "abstinent" or "celibate" because they were not having "penis in vagina" penetration. However, they consent to oral and anal because they considered them a loophole that "didn't count". Beyond the title, it's important to assess the heart and the intent of your stance concerning your own sexual commitments.

Practicing celibacy and abstinence often requires a lot of effort! Many people who live successful sex-absent lifestyles often do so by maintaining a system of nature defying habits and behaviors that include but aren't limited to these methods: suppressing response to pleasure, avoiding physical touch, denying erotic connection, and repelling thoughts and behaviors that are associated with sex. After many years of seemingly perfecting anti-sex antics, many people struggle to undo all the work they've done to distance themselves from organic arousal. I could write an entire book on this topic. I've been there! A lot of married women tend to struggle with this. They arrive to the one place where sexual conviction isn't required and sometimes struggle to undo all the work they've done. If you can relate to this, I'd advise you to identify how those practices served you in the past and how they may influence your current sex life. Ask yourself, "What sexual acts or ideas give me the most pause?" and consider why. If your answers are minor or you can't think of any, decide to address those things and maybe even discuss them with your spouse. A simple decision to unlearn the practices associated with your singleness can open up a lot of sexual possibilities in your marriage. I find that a lot of the conversation centered around celibacy and abstinence is based on each individual's perception of the terms.

Despite whether you practice it or not, what is your understanding of celibacy and abstinence?

REPRODUCTION

Each time a man ejaculates, he releases an average of 20 million to 100 million sperm cells (some dudes shoot like cowboys while others barely pull the trigger). In addition to that, females are born with an average of about two million eggs, and approximately 1,000 die every month. A man can accidentally precum more seed in one occurrence than a woman is even born with. During each menstrual cycle, a woman releases, on average, one mature egg. Sometimes she can release more than one, which can cause multiple births if each of the eggs are fertilized. In spite of the science, we've reduced this information to a cliché quote, "If you have sex, you can get pregnant." That phrase scares the living daylights out of some and inspires hope in others, but the fact of the matter is it doesn't always work that way.

Every time you lie down, you are not necessarily trying to reproduce. That's not how our reproductive organs even work anyway. I say "necessarily" because, for women trying to conceive, reproduction is an ever-present thought. In one of the interviews I conducted for this book, a woman described her frustrations with infertility and the fact that she and her husband have not yet been able to conceive a child. I say "not yet" because she and her husband haven't given up faith. Even as I write this, I stand in faith that they will one day become parents. They've tried different positions, natural herbs and remedies, changed their diets, had him examined, and even worked with a fertility specialist to no avail.

She looked me dead in my eyes and said, "We've been trying diligently for four years. Do you know how much sex that adds up to?"

I sat silently. I tried to think of something to say—perhaps a joke to lighten the mood—maybe an actual estimate. Seconds continued to pass, and the words didn't find their way to my lips. My inability to produce an answer wasn't strong enough to break her gaze, and I'm confident that's exactly the response she wanted me to provide. Silence.

"And while four years is long, you know what's longer?" she shot. Silence again. My stomach felt uneasy, and a lump began to grow in my throat. As a mother of two kids who seemed to have popped up out of thin air in a desirable but effortless fashion and timeframe, I was reminded that this is not everyone's story. I was counting my blessings while empathetically talking with a woman that trusted me with this very personal and vulnerable part of her journey. "Forty-eight months," she continued. "Forty-eight periods, and 48 reminders that I'm still not pregnant."

The lump in my throat felt like a watermelon, and the weight of the moment was heavy. I felt jittery. For a moment, it felt as if her pain had pulled up a chair and sat at the table with us. We sat together in that moment, the three of us. She went on to detail about how people's well-intended "Just pray about it," "It's going to happen," or "When yall gon' have a baby?" comments felt like salt being poured on an open wound. I was humbled by her story and angered at the same time. We're so used to not talking about sensitive and taboo topics that it enables people, in general, to make thoughtless comments while simultaneously removing the opportunity for those who are affected to share their stories. I decided at that moment that I would be a proponent of changing the narrative one way or another.

An average of about 15% of pregnancies end in miscarriage within the first trimester[1]. Additionally, about 20% of women struggle with fertility in one fashion or another. I would include the statistic on abortion rates, but accurate reporting on the average number of abortions performed annually was inconsistent across several sources. Needless to say, every attempt to conceive doesn't end with a bouncing healthy baby. That's a tough reality, but it's true! It's even tougher living in a world that seems to function as if this isn't the case.

In the process of conducting interviews, I was astonished by what I discovered about women I knew *personally*. Some had lost children and/or had struggle(d) with infertility, but we never had that conversation before. Some of the most common conversational threads amongst these women were the feelings of loneliness and despair. You really feel like you're all alone, especially when all you see are babies everywhere—reminders of other people's successful pregnancies. They're on the commercials, in the stores, in our neighborhoods, our families, our churches, everywhere. However, what we don't see are all of the babies of our hearts. The miscarried, the deceased, the aborted, the ones yearned for and aren't here ... the ones who will never make their appearances on this side of eternity. No one sees the invisible babies, but talking about them may help the women who can relate. This is yet another way we can connect with one another and reduce the distance between us—talking. One of the key weapons or strategies that an enemy can use against us is isolation. Isolation physically and mentally can create a considerable distance between us and our creativity, our goals, our peace, and our purpose at any turn. It can keep us distanced from each other.

The ever-present mental bubble of reproduction can be a cloud in the sky of sexual bliss. Although sex is most commonly the primary pathway to reproduction (aside from in-vitro, surrogacy, cloning, or other creative methods not on my immediate radar), mentally sex and reproduction should hold their own specific mental space to preserve the integrity of both. Sex is an opportunity to connect with your partner. It should be pleasurable. It should be fun. It should be consensual. If you're worried about getting pregnant or not getting pregnant, you may forfeit the full potential of the moment. For the sake of not sacrificing that full potential, a lot of times, people play "Russian Roulette" by engaging in unprotected, unprohibited sex and choose to deal with the ramifications later...whatever they may be.

How has the fear of getting pregnant or the pain of not conceiving affected your perception of sex? How do you think these factors impact other people (men vs. women)?

THE HUMAN BODY

I remember my first working car, a 1992 Saturn. I loved that little car; it got the job done! However, it had a few things that weren't in optimal shape, and from time to time, it could be annoying, to say the least. If you accidentally opened the sunroof, it would be stuck open for days because the button only worked once every blue moon within a leap year. Also, the seals on the doors had served their time and retired, I guess, so every time it rained, I would get drenched from my left shoulder down to my feet. It was so bad I learned to tuck a trash bag just at the rim of my collar and drape it onto my clothes so I could at least arrive to my destination partially dry. It drank oil like a toddler mid-play break on a sunny day. I could go on and on about that car and all the lovely hurdles we crossed together, but one thing I could say is that it ran! It got me from point A to point B, and that was all that mattered. Likewise, for our bodies.

Despite the things we understand, like, and dislike, the fact that we're alive is an accomplishment in and of itself. I know that may not mean much to someone tired of living, but it could also mean the world to someone who feels like my little hooptie and their parts aren't quite seeming to "work right." I want to encourage that person and those people and let them know that their worth is not minimized to the functions of their body or the lack thereof. It never has been, and it never will be. Sure, those things may be mentioned from time to time, or even all the time, but you have the opportunity to move forward knowing these things are only mere parts of your story and not the whole book. You must separate the two!

"What you don't know won't hurt you" is a quote I've heard spoken many times before in an attempt to justify secrecy or replace full transparency. It seemed to make sense when I heard it, and even when I used it until I truly thought about it. While it can be necessary for various reasons, ignorance can also hurt you a great deal, even if you are unaware of the "pain" or harm it has truthfully caused. This is why therapy and counseling can be key parts of understanding your thoughts and feelings. As the taboo of "seeking help" loses its power, more and more people are considering giving it a try and attempting to sort through their thoughts and experiences with an unbiased party and that is powerful! It takes a certain level of self-awareness and humility to admit that there's some thing or things that need to be addressed. That's the very power of seeking help, it's one's availability. It's easier to take hold of an open hand as opposed to a clenched fist. It begins with a posture of readiness. Back in the day, getting help held the stigma that you were "crazy" or in some way "not well". With that stigma, people chose to live out the ramifications of those stigmas for fear of seeking help and having them actually confirmed. Nowadays, people are starting to view it as a sign of strength and true self reflection. It seems like everyone is running to find a therapist/counselor as we realize that life has some unique ways of screwing us up—all of us. More and more people are seeking assistance in getting their monsters from under the bed and skeletons out of their closets. There isn't enough room for these things to take up as much space in our lives as they have for ages. Again, these conversations are liberating and provide access to clarity and deeper insight.

THERE'S NO ONE LIKE YOU

I recognize that being different is sometimes a very isolating position, but regarding our personal stories in combination with our specific anatomical makeup, there is simply no one like you. Like fingerprints, so are our minds—and vaginas. Each and every individual is unique and sport the trophies and battle wounds of life that prove it! This is relevant because if you're not mindful of our differences, you may feel like something is wrong with you. In one of my very candid girlfriend chats, we randomly ended up talking about sex positions. We both had somehow assumed that we would favor the same positions, especially since we had similar body types. I know that doesn't make sense now, but in the moment it made total sense to both of us. Well, that couldn't have been further from the truth. One woman's favorite is another woman's snooze. One woman's "go-to" was another's "What is that?" We laughed and shared honestly but still with a bit of reserve. As much as we had talked and shared over the years, somehow, we seemed to miss this conversation. We took a moment to specifically discuss our preferences in terms of position and effect, and we both felt enlightened by the end of the conversation. We both walked away with new and specific context about how we had "mastered" some of our preferences.

How do you think the choice to not engage in certain thoughts about anatomy and sex have impacted your life? How do you go about seeking information about sexual pleasure? What do you think is the impact of not seeking

new information about sex? If you wanted to learn something new today, what would your go-to source be and why? Have you considered therapy/counseling and do you think that decision impacts your perspective concerning sex?

CHAPTER 5: IS THIS NORMAL?

 If you're always trying to be normal, you will never know how amazing you can be."

— MAYA ANGELOU

Prior to writing this book, I never would've imagined some of the things I've heard from women about their bodies, perspectives, and the shame or embarrassment sometimes associated with both. Often, when asked who else they've talked to about the various topics, I was surprised to learn I was sometimes the only one. From third and fourth nipples to sensationless and calloused nerve endings, sometimes search engines fail us when we don't quite know what to search. If a situation is already rare to begin with, finding the precise words to trigger an algorithm in a search engine is darn near impossible.

Naturally, differences require unique attention. In a field full of thousands of yellow flowers, your eye will undoubtedly be drawn to the one red flower amongst them. That's just the way it is. So when it comes to our bodies, we are both intentionally and unintentionally hyper-aware of the things that seem common and those that do not. It's difficult to determine what's common when a lot of our thoughts and ideas about sex and our bodies are hidden and/or "dressed up." Plainly put, nothing is "wrong" with you. There is and has only ever been one of you. You're a special edition! Naturally, you are different, and that's "normal."

Now some things may not function as expected or maybe even require "special" attention, but you are not a broken vessel. This chapter is special to me because I truly believe a lot of things will be set straight. Several chains will be broken, and hearts and minds will be put at ease. Even if you're not necessarily the person who can "benefit," you may be the person who can help someone by simply being able to say, "I've heard of that before." Sometimes we think something is "wrong" when it doesn't function the way we expected, if it exceeds our expectations, or if it's just plain...different.

I remember having my first child and learning to breastfeed. While some mamas struggled with milk production and wondering, "Is my baby getting enough?" I was a whole "Bessy the Cow" over here. My friend and I took our infants on a walk one day, and my breasts got so engorged I had to stop and "wring 'em out" off to the side of the path. I felt like I had no choice because my breasts were rock solid, my daughter wasn't hungry, and I was in pain! In retrospect, I could've prepared and addressed the situation differently. Ounce after ounce dripped on the concrete right between me and my stroller. Relief! I wasted at least four ounces on the spot—and that was per boob!

No one I knew at that time produced as much milk as I did, not to mention I was one of the first women in my immediate circle who was exclusively breastfeeding. I hardly knew what I was doing. It wasn't until I met another "Bessie" in a mom class who shared a story of her boobs "shooting out milk" after her baby unlatched that I felt a little more "normal." "Me too!" I shouted. She and I connected immediately! This poor girl shared stories of darn near drowning her daughter with her abundance of milk and waking up practically swimming in a pool of her own milk if she went too long without nursing! We connected in a way that we hadn't with anyone else prior to that point on that topic. It was powerful! Dare I say revolutionary. This connection was brought about by us taking a moment to verbalize our stories candidly, vulnerably, and honestly. After connecting with her and other stories like ours, I learned more about my liquid gold producing breasts and how to take advantage of their strength. I went on to breastfeed for more than a year after that. The point of the story is that I found comfort in being able to relate to someone else. Whatever it is, chances are, you are not alone. The key is to figure out how to access other peoples stories, but that oftentimes comes at the risk of sharing yours.

NORMALCY

It's common to hide behind a shield of normalcy to protect ourselves from being embarrassed, or perhaps, ostracized by information we simply cannot redact. Cover-ups, concealers, and facades are all fair game when trying to hide something. Insinuations, "You know what I mean," and head nods somehow become a coded language while truth remains choked within us—snuggly tucked between our breasts, vulnerability and true liberty.

How do you tend to ask deeply personal questions (about sex or otherwise), and who do you ask? What's the risk of asking the questions it seems hardest to ask? Is the risk of initiating these conversations worth it? Why is appearing "normal" sometimes more important than the actual truth of our differences?

I remember the first time I had an orgasm; I went to the bathroom and shed a tear of joy and breathed a sigh of relief! I'm laughing even as I type this, but that is the actual truth! Excited is an understatement! You see, prior to that moment I didn't really know what I was missing nor how to even begin to access it. However, the control freak in me had figured out a way to let my guard down—to let pleasure direct the ship, and that was an accomplishment for me! The neatest part in me had found a narrow hole of sloppiness, and I was rolling in it like a pig in a pen. You see, prior to having that orgasm, I had decided that my vagina was broken. Something was most certainly wrong with me because I knew the path I was traveling went much further. I seemed to get stuck at a familiar stopping point every time. Mentally, I just couldn't seem to commit and follow through. Now, as vocal as I am, I had never told anyone aside from my husband about my broken vagina while it was still broken— how do you start that conversation?

"Hey 'So-and-So,' I think my vagina's broken," or "Excuse me, ma'am, what aisle do you guys store your broken vagina cream?"

No way! No how! Not me, and I for darn sure wouldn't have imagined actually publishing that in a book for the world to read—yet here we are. Ahhhh, life is pure comedy isn't it? At that time, I valued people *assuming* I was having earth-shattering, recording-breaking orgasms more than *experiencing* them. Not only that, but with so many signals pointed toward sex around me, the thought hadn't occurred to me that others were experiencing or had experienced the same thing. This had me even further convinced that my girl was *really* broken.

I eventually found the words along with the courage to navigate my very soul and figure out what was going on within me. You see, not only was that my lived experience but my automatic response was to yield to it as a "problem" instead of being proactive and diligent enough to seek a solution. I had to be willing to "talk about it" with myself first. I knew there was a solution between me and the information I needed, I just had to find a bridge. I just couldn't seem to "let it go," if you will. Where's Elsa when you need her? Armed with a new sense of security created by transparency, I began to take a more deliberate initiative to listen to my body and organically respond to both my mental and physical state in real-time. I had to figure out a way to be fully present and somewhat selfish. I now realize it wasn't selfish at all, but that's what I thought at the time and it helped. That in and of itself was a great feat (especially since I had practically mastered the art of caring for others before myself with life in general). I became more familiar with my body, my feelings, and my overall state of being. The dam of overthinking broke and seemed to dissipate just enough for pleasure to take the lead. Patience and intention won that battle for me, but I realize everyone's story is different. Some people may need patience, intention, therapy, or maybe even medical attention, and that's ok, too! Girl, be relentless in getting what you need! Some aspects of our lives and bodies simply require more of our attention. Whether its a "problem" or you're just looking to enhance something that is functioning pretty well, my advice is the same. Be it your mind or your body, you *must* take the time necessary to take care of yourself. Always! Be present, observant and proactive about getting what you need to live your best life!

It is also important to realize that the human body is a fascinating work of art! The muscles in your pelvic floor contract and relax depending on how comfortable, relaxed, or aroused you are. I remember around the time of my first pap smear. I'd heard friends and acquaintances talk about their experiences, but they all were so different. Some talked about getting a pap smear like it was as simple as getting your temperature taken, while others described it like giving birth in terms of discomfort or pain. I didn't know what to expect or where I would fall on that spectrum, but I knew I would eventually find out. At the doctor's office, I was very calm. The atmosphere was inviting, my doctor was kind, and the nurse was relatable. All these factors dismantled all of the ideas that could've made that experience scary. The doctor talked me through the entire process.

"I'm going to touch you now," she said as she felt around down there. "I'm going to insert the speculum now; you're going to feel a little pressure," she prepared me.

It wasn't painful to me at all. The most painful part of the process was that I became awkwardly aware of my hands. "Where do I put them?" I thought to myself. "Where do other people put their hands?" I hadn't a clue. I then tried putting them in different positions. I crossed them on my chest, but I felt like a corpse in a casket, so I took them off. Then I put them on my knees, but that felt weird. I went on to struggle with the thought of where my hands should go for what seemed like an eternity until the end of my exam. I truly felt like she should've just told me where to put them before she started; she was narrating everything else. Just goofy! I was glad when it was over. As if that wasn't weird enough, I went on to do the hand dance for several years. I wouldn't think about my hands like ever—in life—until I was in the waiting room. "Crap," I'd think to myself, "Where will they end up today?" Anyways, the point of that ever so random story was that my vagina or the "discomfort" of the exam was the least of my concerns. While my exams were always "light and easy" (minus the hands thing), I realize the experience is much different for many people.

Making sex mutually fulfilling for both men and women should be the norm, but in society we find that difficult to do without blurring the lines between what is "appropriate" for a woman and what is not. For example, taking the lead during sex may feel out of place to a woman who feels that the man should always maintain that position. There is so much misinformation concerning sexual gender roles that we've unintentionally created a culture of mediocrity concerning sex. If you don't believe that fact, then maybe you believe that we live amongst a culture of sexual excellence. A place where all parties are knowledgeable and living their best sex lives. After much thought, study, and investigation, I've come to the conclusion that we live amongst a community of "just enough." We *should* be living in the world of ecstasy and discovery that sex makes possible. Sex is *amazing*! It's powerful, fun, and schedule/life-altering. I can barely write this darn book because of life, two kids, and ... research. I can't tell you the countless situations in which women are taught, coached, and convinced that sex is and should be about the man—his pleasure and his experience. It's not usually direct though. It's concealed in statements like, "What you don't do, another woman will" or "Men are visual, so you have to keep yourself up." I'm all for encouraging women to meet their man's needs, but let's be clear: I'm even more passionate about my sisters getting theirs so both parties' needs can be met! I'm all about being "eye candy," but that sweet delight goes both ways. Far too often, statements are made that are geared exclusively toward meeting a man's erotic needs.

What terms, quotes, or bits of advice have you heard that are exclusive toward a man's sexual satisfaction? How have those statements had an impact on your perspective...if at all? Can you think of parallel advice given to men?

HURDLES

So, what exactly is standing between you and your personal development? Let's get down to business. Again, if you can't think of anything to discuss here, then your position in this moment is that of a listener and a bridge for someone else— your friend, sister, mother, daughter, fellow vagina possessor. These women will have an opportunity to educate others as well, including their partners. Therefore, you have the unique opportunity to impact the overall sex culture in a meaningful way. How exciting!

One of the most important parts of inquiry is the empowerment to investigate. Far too often, we just take things as they are. It seems that we don't always realize that things can actually get better. Even things that are good can be improved. When it comes to our bodies and sex, sometimes the conversations just never seem to come up. It's up to you to bring them up! Sure, partners and other people can play a role in you living your best life, but the major stakeholder in that process is you!

One way to dismantle a false narrative is to find the thread of truth and standardize it first. There are several hurdles that thwart productive, conducive, and healthy conversations about sex, it is essential to identify the factors that affect you the most. There are common factors like time, personality and values. There are power structures like patriarchy, gender roles, and governmental influence. In addition, there are personal ones like self esteem, health and restrictions. Honestly, the list of hurdles that could impact our individual mindsets and journeys is vast. Sometimes your life and personal journey may serve as a hurdle in its own unique way.

It's not surprising that hurdles can also restrict or influence the conversation altogether. From mental blocks associated with various experiences, to thoughts and perhaps fears that cause much excitement or shame. Hurdles take on a variety of forms.

What do you think are some of the common and less common hurdles that women deal with in having conversations about sex? What are some of the things you think women find most difficult to discuss? What are some of your hurdles?

PHYSICAL DIFFERENCES

While penises commonly have the opportunity to exist externally and are visually a bit more "accessible" out front, vaginas are "tucked" in and "concealed" a little bit more. We can categorize penises into three categories: length, girth, and shape (no, not all of them are straight). But vaginas? Oh, girl, I can't begin to categorize them, and believe me, I tried. Unlike the penis, the vagina isn't a singular shaft. It's made up of several different parts: the labia majora and minora (inner and outer lips), the clitoris, the clitoral hood, the vaginal opening, and don't get me started on the inside! The woman's crotch area and its varying parts is a whole book in and of itself!

If I were forced to try, though, I would start by exclusively examining the variations in size between the anatomical differences. Some parts can be small to seemingly non-existent, while others can be simultaneously quite pronounced. These differences, in addition to one's partner's anatomy, can significantly affect one's sexual experience. Understanding your own body is the key to being able to communicate and/or duplicate experiences. Then you and/or your partner can manipulate them to enhance your pleasure in future experiences. I can't tell you the number of times a client has told me about their partner repeatedly doing "what worked for others" or transparently "something they watched in porn". Time after time these women went along with acts that didn't achieve their desired attempt because they couldn't quite describe what actually would "do it for them".

A simple familiarity task is to grab a mirror and examine yourself. Think about it; men see their penises every day—

multiple times a day when they pee (and whatever other reasons they find to look at it)! We don't get a direct peek when we go to the bathroom, so we would have to be a bit more intentional about seeking familiarity with our appearance than our male counterparts. Seeing your vagina can alert you to information about yourself that you may not be aware of.

How often do you think women, on average, pull back the curtains with a mirror and see what's going on down there (try to name a percentage)? Do you think women of faith are less prone to be self-aware? Why or why not? Have you or do you examine your vagina with a mirror? If not, why? If so, how often?

HIS AND HER EQUIPMENT

There is no standard-sized penis or vaginal opening. The hymen in a vagina is usually a thin membrane found over the vagina opening. However, sometimes it's more pronounced, and other times it's completely absent. In one of my "candid chats," a woman described a situation where her hymen was so pronounced that she had to have it cut open by a doctor. Now, she knew this because a doctor informed her, but imagine unsuccessfully "attempting" to be penetrated by a penis and not knowing why it wasn't happening. Penetration by a speculum for pap smear or even a tampon were impossible for her prior to the hymenectomy. When the vagina is penetrated for the first time, it often causes bleeding, but it sometimes doesn't. The hymen can be broken in various ways: horseback riding, tampon insertion, even doing the splits--the list goes on and on. Sometimes the break isn't even noticed. There are whole cultures and communities that celebrate the bleeding of a woman to "confirm" the maintenance of her virginity, but the two are not always synonymous.

PAIN/DISCOMFORT

Simply put, everything doesn't feel "good" all the time. It's not supposed to. When it comes to sex, pain and discomfort can occur in different ways. The highest leverage move in addressing this is being observant as to when, why and how this dissatisfactory sensation occurs. While there are different layers and causes, let me take this moment to encourage self awareness. Pay attention to your body! There are hormonal cycles that our bodies use to give us clues about what's going on with us. Keep a journal or a cycle tracking app to organize your thoughts. Note changes in the way you feel, perhaps the amount discharge or lack thereof and your sexual interactions. You can even note significant events in life as stress and other health related topics commonly impact the way your body functions and reacts.

Don't believe every myth. Just because you're wet that doesn't mean you're horny; likewise, if you're dry, that doesn't automatically mean you're not. Vaginal wetness can indicate arousal; however, there are times where this isn't the case. Vaginal lubrication is a result of increased blood flow to the genital area, which produces vaginal discharge inside of the vaginal walls. Vaginal discharge is a blanketed term that refers to all the stuff that comes out of the vagina: ejaculate, mucus, blood, uterine lining, "wetness", and more. Vaginal discharge varies from person to person at different times as well. This is why it's important to note your particular circumstance in order to use the information you've gathered for your benefit. Regardless of what your body is or isn't doing, I can provide a universally accurate recommendation for everyone: Drink water! Stay hydrated! You need it anyway, but so does your vagina.

Lube, lube, lube! In addition to our natural lubrication, personal lubricants fill the store shelves for a reason! Buy it (and thank me later). Lubrication is not some crutch or training wheel, it's a tool for your tool belt. You can use some over the counter lube, natural oils or even spit. During sex, the pumping and the movement of air can sometimes evaporate and cause what was once wet and slippery to become a little dryer and uncomfortable. Lube up! The wetter, the better! The friction created between our bodies during intercourse is can be a glorious thing, but without proper lubrication it can burn a cat up! You don't have to endure pain or discomfort helplessly in any regard! Ask questions and be bold about taking care of your body and mindset.

I know being neat is often the norm, but sex gets messy—and that's ok. Even mentally, sex requires creativity to create, maintain, and enhance excitement. That creativity lies in who you are, what you like and what's going on in your life. Consider your career or field of experience and how that may influence your sexual preferences. Someone working in the service industry for example may have a higher value for exceptional "service" and being served. I know it can seem a little irrelevant, but when it comes to sex nothing is off the table. Take the information you collect about yourself and add it to foreplay. Sex shouldn't be uncomfortable, but the reality is that sometimes it is. Some positions, angles, and situations are not best suited for you or your body type. Lack of familiarity with yourself and your body can present the perfect opportunity for discomfort. Don't be afraid to get proactive! Take inventory on what's going on and get to work on seeking ways to address it.

CHILDBIRTH

I had a c-section with my first child but delivered my second vaginally. My vagina tore a little with my vaginal delivery (as some women do). There are varying degrees of tearing. A first degree tear means there was a minor/surface tear that wasn't "too bad". The most severe is a fourth degree tear which means a woman split from what I like to describe as the "rooter to the tooter". This means the tear goes from the vagina all the way to the anus. Mine was labeled second degree, it wasn't exactly "minor" but I survived it. Thoughts of sex postpartum can be kind of scary...at least it was for me. Having your entire midsection cut open or vaginal opening sewn back together were not exactly "mood setting" events for me. Now I know some women can't wait to "get back at it", but that wasn't my story. I had to be patient with myself. I had to ease my way back into the "swing of things." I didn't know how sex would feel once the doctors recommend six weeks had come to a close. Doctors recommend an average of six weeks without penetration to allow your body to heal and also to create a doctor's order of "rest" for women that would otherwise not be granted such. Some people may heal faster than prescribed, while others need much more time. Remember everyone's body is different. It's important to listen to your body and be self-aware during that time—and any time for that matter.

More than discomfort or pain, there are several contributing factors that could hinder pleasure. The range is vast; it's important to pay attention to what is happening and when. Then try to find the words to express it so you can seek answers. Likewise for pleasure. Pay attention to the "good stuff" so you can duplicate, modify and replicate it in future experiences. The key to both is self awareness. The perfect recipe is to reduce the unfavorable while actively increasing the favorable. I know it sounds simple, but I can't tell you how many women come to me for advice about sex and one of our immediate findings is a lack of balance in that idea.

Concerning pain or discomfort, take a moment to identify the factors contributing to your situation so you can put the experience into words. If this is an unfamiliar process for you I encourage you to try as much as possible. Words describing discomfort may not sound "sexy" but eventually it may get you to a place where you can more accurately describe an experience or sensation and its location. It will help you to request the increase or decrease of specific interactions and concepts. Afterward, devise a plan of execution. Talk to your partner, make adjustments, seek advice or medical attention. Discharge, yeast infections, urinary tract infections, sexually transmitted diseases and infections, hormonal imbalances, Polycystic Ovarian Syndrome, vaginismus, menopause, anatomical variances ... the list is never-ending. There are many reasons why sex can be uncomfortable or even painful. Sometimes you may experience more than one simultaneously. It happens! It's ok! Your only job is to educate yourself and actively seek out solutions...and there are solutions by the way. Girl, there is nothing new under the sun. In addition to the physical hindrances I mentioned, there may also be mental ones.

Mental walls built of shame, ignorance, and restraint that prevent the liberty that truly belongs to you. You might be experiencing a combination of both. God created sex, and it is a beautiful. It can be a beautiful display of worship within a marriage covenant and also an invasive weapon used against individuals for selfish gain. I believe we should thoroughly discuss both extremes and every single layer in between. A larger theme I want to highlight is that sex itself is not innately bad. It is beautiful, majestic, and euphoric, and it should be respected as such. It is sin that we hate, violation that we despise, and perversion that we unanimously abhor. Separation is necessary to rightly judge it all.

Due to the nature of this book, people have reached out, recommended books/resources, and sought out my expertise about several things sex-related. The inquiries I'm most passionate about are the cries for help! One phone call stands out to me at this moment. A friend called me the night after her wedding asking for advice because her husband's penis wouldn't "fit" the night before. She was a virgin, she was nervous, and she had no clue what to do. She needed help—she asked for *my* help! The most interesting thing to me is that she had a team of active women in her life who loved her, but none of them had prepared her for this moment. They missed it! I don't even think I got an invitation to the wedding, now there I was talking about the "afterparty." I totally get it by the way, wedding guest lists can be complicated.

Ladies, let's not miss it when it comes to the women entrusted to our specific circles and communities. We must shift the culture of conversation! She and I were friends, but I wouldn't have expected her to come to me for help at that moment when she had so many other accessible women. She was calling from the airport bathroom on the way to her honeymoon. We were able to talk and she was able to ask questions and get some tips on starting her new life. Of all the advice I was able to give her, the most pertinent was that I encouraged her to communicate with her partner above all. Try to be confident, relaxed and honest about what she was feeling. It's not uncommon for the first time to "hurt" or be a bit uncomfortable. This was her situation. Some people continue to experience discomfort until they get a little more used to being sexually active. On the flip side, some people experience little to no discomfort at all. If pain or discomfort persists for you, take note, make adjustments and don't be afraid to seek medical attention if you feel like something isn't "right". By the way...they figured things out, and they're having a blast now.

LIBIDO

Your libido is essentially your sexual desire or lack thereof. The topic of sex drive is an interesting one. At times, your libido is so high you can't seem to get enough, then there are times where the last thing you want to do is even think about being touched. One's sex drive is comprised of mental, physical, and circumstantial factors. Your hormones play a big role in how frisky you feel. If the hormones aren't the ones to start the party, your mind can get things going from your senses or pure imagination; the mind is a powerful place. Lastly, circumstance is a significant one. It's not necessarily at the forefront of our minds, but what I find attractive and enticing is not the same as what women in another culture, like position, geographic location or era may find sexy.

It's not unusual for our sex drives to fluctuate; in fact, it's healthy. It's important to be aware of just how much and why, though. If you're aware of your body, mind, and preferences, you can manipulate them for your benefit. Far too often, people live sex lives full of situations they "stumble" across. If we don't take our own information into account, we may unintentionally assign credit or blame to factors or people we shouldn't.

How would you describe your overall sex drive? Is your sex drive consistent, more often high, low, or consistently fluctuating? What factors do you think most commonly affect ones' sex drive? What questions do you have concerning libido?

RIGHT VERSUS WRONG

I'll simply say, "The marriage bed is undefiled," for my Bible-believing readers. What you and your partner agree to do is between God and the two of you. Lust, hyper-sexualization, and perceived carelessness from women have been shunned in varying degrees for ages. In effort to avoid even the likeness of these things, certain habits, traditions, and even criticisms have been engrafted into society and popular culture. There's a subconscious image of a wife; then there's another image of a "sex symbol." While women are often taught to aspire to be a neat "wife type," there is the constant reminder of the sex symbol and how she seems to be the winner of sexual affection. How can one successfully entice her husband without mastering the art of allure? We've seen this situation many times before, the neat Mother Teresa type woman remains single yet desires companionship, while Marilyn Monroe over here is working on husband number four. There is a wide gap between being sexy and being a saint...but it doesn't have to be.

Attaching a woman's worth to her body is misleading in that, over time, she may believe that the most precious dynamic of her worth is exclusively associated with the sex she does or does not have. Sit with that for a moment. Do you associate your worth with your sex life? I assure you, your worth includes a lot more than this aspect of your life. This is also what makes sexual abuse even more egregious! Not only is sexual abuse a violation against one's will, but according to the aforementioned concept, it also is the definition of robbing someone of his or her entire worth if this is the standard they intentionally or unintentionally live by.

BOUNDARIES

While the formation of boundaries concerning sex stretch far and wide, it's important for you to consider the factors that contribute to the setting of your boundaries or lack thereof. It is of the utmost importance to assess your circumstance and have a clear understanding of your foundation and if you are intentionally upholding ideas that you have chosen as opposed to ones impressed on you. When you arm yourself with the awareness of clarity concerning your boundaries, you can choose to maintain or abandon certain ideas depending on your own motivations. You don't have to live a sex life being carted off into someone else's fantasy at rocket speed, but realistically this happens all of the time. You have a voice and part of using that voice is figuring out what you're even trying to say.

In one of my "candid chats," I spoke with a woman who had never been kissed before the man who ultimately became her husband. While this was her experience, he, on the other hand, had lost count of the women he had sex with. Although he was patient and kind, there was a significant gap between their expectations and boundaries. The things that made her "clutch her pearls" were no big deal to him as he had experienced them countless times before. The things that she considered a "special treat" were less than ordinary to him. Her complaints of life and keeping up and his desires for her to be sexier or meet his needs and sexual appetite often clashed as they had yet to intentionally acknowledge the gap between them and devise a realistic and manageable plan to address it. They avoided talking about sex "too much" to avoid being tempted or inappropriate during their courtship, so neither of them knew just how far apart in knowledge and expectation they truly were.

Likewise, in another "candid chat," I spoke with a woman who shared a much more comparable sex history as her husband and their previous partners. Still, the boundaries between her and her partner were different based on knowledge and preference. Because she was in the nursing field, her restrictions were centered around cleanliness and anatomy. One of the topics she brought up was anal sex. While her husband had done it and wanted to try it with her, it was NEVER going to happen. That was a hard boundary for her. Anal sex for her partner was conventional and no big deal, but it stood as a hard line for her, so they don't do it. She took a moment and vividly explained the sphincter muscle, pudendal nerve, and pelvic floor, and I took notes. I had never heard of a lot of the stuff she was talking about, and a lot of people haven't but her career allowed her to obtain information over the years that most people aren't necessarily thinking about. The beauty in the moment was that her ability to articulate her boundaries gave me as a girlfriend access to knowledge I didn't have before. Concerning her sexual journey, her knowledge about anal sex superseded her desire to explore and discover in that regard, although her spouse would prefer that it didn't. The bottom line is, you have an obligation to set your own boundaries and hard lines.

It's important to note that our individuality is one of the most precious aspects of our lived experience. From our mindsets to our anatomy, all parts of us are "normal" to us. You must honor that. From that mindset, be empowered to make decisions, seek knowledge, and consider different aspects of your sex life and body.

CHAPTER 6: TWISTED MINDS AND THEIR TRAILS OF RESIDUE...

 One's dignity may be assaulted and vandalized, but it can never be taken away unless it's surrendered."

— MEGAN FOX

Often sexual abuse is viewed as the "victim's shame" instead of the "culprit's crime." I have a *huge* problem with that, and you should, too. Whether we have experienced sexual abuse or not, we are all, in one way or another, advocates navigating our involvement in the conversation of sexual abuse. Don't let people get away with saying and doing "dumb stuff" or exhibiting carelessness just because. As a bystander, make the commitment to challenge these words and actions when and how you can. Advocacy is scary when thinking of doing it in an uncomfortable or unnatural way. It's not reasonable to ask a shy person to shout, or the poor to sacrifice what little funds they have. So, don't think of it that way. Use whatever resources you have to address the injustices occurring around you. That's all anyone can ask of you. No one wants to be the person who is "doing too much," but at what cost? To avoid "doing too much," you could run the risk of not doing enough, and that's not ok.

Your counter or rebuke of an inappropriate comment or mindset may save a life...or several. Every abuser comes from somewhere. These folks aren't just dropping out of the sky. They're a part of families, communities, neighborhoods ... *our* families, communities and neighborhoods. They need to hear and be exposed to the fact that their lustful cravings and lack of self-control should not overpower their ability to think rationally and respect others. We must hold each other accountable when we can.

Isn't it in the least bit "odd" that there are so many people we know and love who have been abused, but we don't know as many abusers? That's because it's not true. We do know the abusers! People aren't as vocal about their toxic sexual behaviors as they are about the toxicity imposed on them (and people tend to be minimally vocal about that as well). The acts are committed, sometimes several times again, yet the assailants tend to be granted the grace of their actions being "alleged." Or better yet, they get the benefit of the doubt: "'So-and-so' wouldn't do anything like that," "That's not like 'So-and-So,'" or "I worked with them." Meanwhile "so and so" is a whole pervert and wreaking havoc in the lives of the people they target. I understand that honesty is not always the standard. Plainly speaking, sometimes people lie, which makes it harder to hold the guilty accountable, but the fact that many people are inclined to automatically side with the accused prior to even gaining full clarity is alarming. I'm not advocating for jumping to conclusions either way, my push is for everyone to be more objective when it comes to these conversations. Don't let your initial instinct be to dismiss. Likewise, don't just take someone's word just because. It is responsible to take a stance of objectivity, which leaves room for truth to prevail. Jumping to conclusions on either side can be equally detrimental. If we shift the culture to holding people accountable for their own thoughts and behaviors in general, we can cultivate a society of more sexually responsible participants.

VIOLATION

Recently, I had a conversation with some friends over brunch, and the topic of sexual abuse came up. One of the women in the group opened up about the sexual abuse that she encountered as a child by a family member. Tearfully and timidly, she leaked out small details about a relative who sexually molested her in her youth: how she felt, who she told, how it still affects her to this day. Immediately the group began to "encourage" her. I say "encourage" lightly because the intent didn't align with the impact. "You should out him to the family," "Confront him now that you're grown," "Press charges." I watched these comments going into one ear like a tunnel and out the other. There was no way she was doing any of those things; I could just tell.

You see, to be violated is to have someone strip away your feeling of power. The consequences of "telling" can seem worse than the actual abuse itself. Some abusers threaten additional harm or lie/blame the person they are abusing. Some spew threats of potential negative possibilities: "If you tell, then whoever tries to hurt me will end up in jail, and you'll have to go into foster care," or "No one will believe you anyway." Some even manipulate the situation by telling the victim if he/she doesn't take the inappropriate behavior further, then they'll reveal details of how they got to where they are, which candidly can sound sort of "sketchy" even if it's not. Sometimes embarrassment or blaming oneself may be a large part of the shame. Thoughts of "How did I let this happen?" or "If I had/had not done 'x,' then 'y' wouldn't have happened" swirl through your mind.

An often-forgotten population of people affected by sexual abuse are the loved ones of the people who an offender has violated. These people live their lives knowing the "secret" and silently blame themselves for not defending their loved ones or somehow "knowing". Sometimes they carry a similar if not equal mental load as a result of the trauma. Don't punish yourself for the sin of someone else. Whether it happened to you, your friend, or your relative, I want you to know you can move forward and take up a mindset of peace despite what happened. You didn't do it! That violation doesn't have the right to torment and paralyze you from moving forward, so don't allow it to.

Living with the mental weight of abuse and all the regret associated with it can be heavy. One of the first things one can do to get healing is first to address the abuse to yourself —not the abuser. I want to make this distinction because the trauma is within you. Your thoughts. Your feelings. Your conscious and subconscious existence. Before you can even confront anyone about anything, you need clarity concerning the confrontation. In many cases, survivors suppress details, feelings, and instincts as a means of self-preservation.

If you can, take a moment of inventory to identify what those things are. Take it in doses that you can withstand, you don't have to rush. Be patient with yourself and only consider the thoughts that you can. What exactly happened? If you can, recall the incident. This may be painful, but suppressing it won't make it go away or feel better. The purpose of recalling the incident(s) is to strip it of its power and divorce the past from the present and the future. Then you can make conscious decisions concerning your life, body, and mental well-being as opposed to being bullied by the pain of a memory securely tucked away in your very soul. You can then seek professional help if you choose to. It's tough to seek an answer if you haven't considered the actual question.

Some people are seemingly "successful" at suppressing thoughts of abuse, while others relive the details almost daily. I encourage you to lift your head and don't cower fearfully to the pain. It doesn't have to have the power to control you! After you recall the incident(s), identify the effect it had/has on you. Call it out! From here you can make thoughtful decisions about what you have the capacity to do in terms of what you want to do with the information you are able to extract.

In what ways has violation or the thought of it affected your life? How has it impacted your decision making or decisions made around you? How did it impact your views on sex and specific sexual interactions? How did you cope? Would you be open to therapy? What steps have you taken to heal? If the aforementioned questions don't directly apply to you, I encourage you to answer them from an analytical standpoint.

At this moment, I think it's highly appropriate to put in a plug for therapy/counseling. Sexual abuse is a delicate and sensitive topic. There is no blanketed solution to provide someone with the help they need, but if you're willing to talk about it you may be able to uncover some life altering information and strategies to reduce the strain that the abuse has caused. Whether you experienced it or someone you love did, you may benefit greatly from seeing someone with the experience of helping tons of other people that have been in your shoes. The bottom line is that while the past can't be changed, there is and will always be hope for the future.

Self check in concerning sexual abuse:

    1. Identify the power imbalance: Acknowledge what happened and understand the fact that it wasn't your fault.

    2. Delegate responsibility and navigate impact: Assess how it impacted you then, and how it impacts your life now.

    3. Assess the damage: Decide to intentionally make healthy shifts in your perspective and take the posture of a survivor.

    4. Move forward: Prioritize healing and devise a plan to achieve it.

You need to seek healing because you deserve it. While remaining scars can still be visible, those weeping wounds don't have to be permanent. Leaving wounds exposed and unaddressed can cause infection, and the result can be even worse than it was to begin with. While we can't change the past, we can control our perspectives in the present and future. Living beneath the shadows of violation is not your lot. Period! Not only that, but hurt people tend to hurt people. Trying not to think about the impact is inadvertently hurting you and everyone around you even more. Your kids can't leave your sight because you're paranoid. Your spouse can't touch you in certain ways because they bring about uncomfortable memories. You can't experience pleasure in some ways because it feels "wrong." Certain seemingly irrelevant details become reminders of the torment. You could be doing something as simple as watching HGTV, and the designer may position furniture in a way that reminds you of the location of the abuse you endured, and you burst into a cold sweat. Not only were you violated then, but now you have the worst gift ever of reliving the trauma time and time again. That ends today! You don't have to live life this way any longer. You are not alone, though often you may feel like it. You can make a decision to end the cycle. Seek help! Like a doctor for the body, we sometimes need to seek a doctor for the brain. Negative stigmas are often attached to therapy and professional help, but don't allow those stigmas to keep you bound. Now is the time! Take possession of the healing that belongs to you!

THE POWER STRUGGLE

Sexual abuse is a broad umbrella term used to describe a myriad of sexual offenses: rape, molestation, assault, manipulation, harassment, and I'm sure there are several others I'm leaving out. One thing that all these forms of abuse have in common is an imbalance of power and or control. These acts can have lasting negative impressions on the targeted individual(s). For purposes of healing, I want to expand the scope for a moment here. Healing is available. Peace is available. The hope you have for the lingering thoughts to no longer bully you is valid. If you have experienced abuse and would like to address the impact it's had on you but you don't know how, consider the following tips: identify the source, delegate the blame appropriately, assess the damage, then set your intentions moving forward. Once you take those steps, the succeeding possibilities are endless.

IDENTIFY THE POWER SOURCE

One of the first things a person can do to heal from the wrong-doing they experienced is acknowledging where the power or control imbalance was. How did the abuser exercise his/her power to his/her advantage? Examining where their power resided provides a small pocket of distance. Use that distance to empower you and your thoughts in this moment. How did they exalt themselves or their position above you? The following questions may be a little difficult to consider but brace yourself and know that the answers to these questions may provide you with the clarity you need to better understand your feelings. Were they older and used fear as a tactic to silence you? Did they use their physical strength to overpower you? Were they the "boss" or a "co-worker" and used your livelihood as an access point? Were they a part of the family or community and used the threat of tarnishing your reputation against you? Did they simply prey on your innocence, vulnerability, or the trust they had established? See if you can identify the source and stare it dead in the face. The fact of the matter is, they used something, and you have to identify what it was.

DELEGATE THE BLAME/RESPONSIBILITY APPROPRIATELY

This thought isn't directly tied to the act and the pain it caused. It isn't about what the survivor could have done, said, or thought differently. It isn't about the identities of the abused. I don't care if you're faithful, faithless, old, or young. The abuse should not have happened! Period! It's inexcusable, and it's ok to consider it as such. You are not to blame! Even if you consider what you could've done differently, it's still not your fault! You didn't violate yourself, so you can't allow yourself to absorb all of the blame. The responsibility of the act belongs to someone else and you need to make room for this truth in order for your heart to be healed. If you want to blame someone or something, blame the fact that the power dynamic was uneven to begin with. Blame the culprit, the lack of surveillance, the timing, the lack of education; however, what you cannot do is blame yourself. If you have blamed yourself, take a moment to forgive yourself and shift the responsibility to its appropriate place or places.

ASSESS THE DAMAGE

This is an opportunity to be real with yourself. After every terrible storm once people come out from their shelter and hiding, one of the first things they do is come out and assess the damage. If you're still locked inside, you can't actually tell how mess havoc the storm has caused. It's only when you take a step and zoom out will you be able to analyze the situation more clearly. Who all was/is involved? Try not to allow damning thoughts to distract you from your goal. The start of the process is acknowledging that no one deserves to be abused, and it was not your fault. From there, address the details bit by bit within yourself. You may have to trace things back if that makes it easier. For example, ask yourself how that occurrence is affecting you today.

So, how has the act impacted you? As I interview people and have heard several stories of sexual abuse, I find that the outcomes are as unique as each individual's personality. Some carry the trauma deep within, and it hinders them from owning their own sexual experiences authentically. In contrast, others carry the trauma outwardly and base their sexual preferences and decisions on what happened to them.

Are there any areas that the residue has leaked into that you didn't realize until now?

This is a hard question to answer because you don't know what you don't know. A way to seek this out is to take an inventory of the ideas and foundational mindsets you have toward sex. Usually behind them are some thoughts and ideas that have snuggled up and planned to reside there permanently.

Are there any acts that you prefer or detest, and can you identify why?

SET YOUR INTENTIONS ON HEALING

This is not the space where we go after abusers for the ultimate revenge (although who can blame you if that was your initial and honest feeling). This is the place of supreme retrieval of power where we *decide* where to go from here. This is not an "action" to do but a "decision" to make. It's a state of being. It requires honesty and thoughtfulness, careful deliberation, and consideration. The primary goal for anyone who has been abused should be healing (even above revenge)—it must be. Get your power back! Only from a place of healing can you pick yourself up and stand. Only from a place of healing can you analyze the situation without it causing you to fold up and crumble. This is the place where you can boldly declare what you want . Go ahead, make a statement if you can. Here, you can use one of these if you'd like:

> *"I want to get rid of the anxiety."*
> *"I want to reclaim my peace."*
> *"I don't want to be paranoid whenever I'm reminded of it."*
> *"I want to get rid of the guilt, shame, or embarrassment."*

I implore you to make a statement because this is the very part you can take to God in prayer and expect to receive it. Again, we know the past cannot be changed, but your present and future are being formed in this very moment. Decide to shed the weight that may have you bound.

Have you ever tried to pray and find yourself at a loss for words? I admit, there have been times when I set my heart to pray, and I don't even know where to begin because the crap I'm trying to pray about is so screwed up. Imagine trying to unpack some layered trauma. The Bible talks about worshipping God in spirit and in truth—this is the truth part. It's hard to hear, "Pray about it," from some well-meaning citizen when you don't even know what angle to take and why. The statement "Just pray about it" can become toxic and dismissive if spoken as a Band-aid instead of a tourniquet. Blood is shooting out everywhere, and someone comes along to place a little cover on it. That thing is going to continue to bring forth much blood. "Just pray about it" is not a magic wand nor a time portal, and as a faithful praying woman, I am here to say it's going to take a little more than a simple prayer. Now don't give up on prayer; I'm just saying you're not crazy for feeling offended if that's all the helper has to offer. You're not a heathen if you prayed, and you still feel the pain. You have to put forth a little more effort and commitment toward analyzing and recognizing what you experienced and what you're feeling as a result to form the words to say. That's the part you take to prayer and apply the word of God to take a step forward. That step becomes steps, then strides, to eventually a full sprint toward the victory that belongs to you.

I watched an interview once about a man who was sexually abused as a child; the abuser always would rub his shoulders down toward his elbow and back up again several times before taking it further. He did that *every ... single ... time.* Today, he can't stand for anyone to touch him that way. If someone does, he tends to respond aggressively. He regrets that he didn't stand up for himself. That he didn't stop it—that he felt he couldn't stop it. So, if anyone touches his shoulders, he feels the need to fight. Ironically, when he gave his life to Christ and came to the altar, this was the first physical contact that the altar-worker made. It was meant as a message of comfort, but it was a reminder of one of the most horrific seasons of his life. The season of his youth when a man his family trusted, who should have never harmed him, penetrated him anally. If you ask anyone who has been sexually abused about his/her experience, they'll undoubtedly mention the manipulation they experienced and how it was rooted in fear in one way or another. This is one of the many reasons why normalizing "consent" for touching one another should absolutely be the norm. From a cordial handshake to a hug, its respectful to make sure that the recipient even wants to be touched.

I'm not going to lie; I sat here thinking of a scripture I could include to uplift this chapter. Something to brighten up, encourage or shift the mood—but I'm not. This is a dark space. This is a hard place, and though I know God to be a healer, I will not overshadow the emotions and feelings that these words may unearth. People turn their backs on God because of how we as a faith community have handled topics like this. You didn't deserve to be violated. They didn't deserve to be violated. If it wasn't you, rest assured it was someone very close to you, which still inadvertently affects you. You have to face your narrative head-on to halt the damaging and lasting residue it has left in your life. No, you won't talk about it, but it influences your sex life. No, you won't talk about it, but you're allowing it to raise your children. No, you won't talk about it, but it prevents you from releasing the tension in your shoulders.

Do you realize you can carry the trauma of sexual abuse in your physical body?

Developing all kinds of diseases and ailments because that thing has you locked up. The healing isn't just mental; it's both physical and spiritual.

FORGIVENESS

Before I tell you to forgive these undeserving scumbags, I want to validate your feelings and reasoning. The thought process that makes forgiveness difficult is very human and not without merit. We use it as a defense mechanism to attempt to prevent similar transgressions and to try to protect ourselves. True enough, that abuser doesn't deserve your forgiveness, but you do. The version of you who can forgive and move forward is an empowered version of yourself who is better equipped to handle your life. You don't have to become the Earth's doormat to be considered "good" in the eyes of God. The path and speed you travel toward forgiveness is up to you. You set the pace! You don't *have* to forgive them and position yourself to be hurt again. You don't *have* to forgive them and forget what happened.

What does forgiveness or lack of forgiveness look like anyway?

Well, if there's an offense and you deliberately don't forgive, then that means the offense has taken up residence in your heart and mind. You have made the decision, consciously or subconsciously, to maintain negative energy, effort, and malice toward a person or an event. The problem with that is that it requires investment, and you've already paid more than you should have to begin with. Choosing not to forgive is giving the situation additional permission to rob you of your peace. The monstrosity can't exist within you on its own. You have to pay for a place for that thing to reside. Recalling the memories, conjuring up the anger, reliving and rehearsing the event repeatedly is torment and just plain exhausting. Sometimes it has the nerve to sneak up on you unsolicited. All the effort put into not forgiving hurts the person doing it, and, frankly, that pain is far too expensive for some pain we don't even want. Nine times out of ten, the aggressor isn't even aware that you are putting so much thought and energy into not forgiving them. It's important to note: sometimes forgiveness takes time, and that is ok. Don't rush into some fake forgiveness to appear to be more noble than you are. True healing allows you access to the keys that open the door to forgiveness, it's a state of being, a posture, a mindset, a position of power. Be patient with yourself; there is no trophy for rushing some fake forgiveness that brings forward no good fruit.

One time, I had a petty grudge against a coworker. While she didn't sexually assault me, her actions did cause me mental anguish, and I had decided she crossed a line I wasn't willing to forgive. She offended me and then went on to live her merry little life. I was livid! I was conflicted! Quite frankly, I was...hurt. If I saw her car in the parking lot, I parked further to avoid even walking in around the same time. If she was in the teachers' lounge, I'd act like I wasn't trying to go there. If she sat at a particular table for professional development, I tried to sit as far as possible away from her. Reflecting on that experience, I realize that I was working really hard to hold on to my offense. Meanwhile, she parked wherever she wanted. She made her copies and heated her lunch in the teachers' lounge as she pleased, and sat in whatever seats were available or convenient for PD. To this day, she never even knew there was an issue, but I can recall how much time I spent just to maintain my position of unforgiveness. When I decided to forgive her, I had to do so in my heart first. It was solely on the inside of me (right next to the offense that she never even knew I took). Sure, I could've broadcasted my offense and declared, "And I forgive you." The problem is that I would've been even more hurt if she responded in a way that I didn't deem good enough.

Forgiveness is truly an act of the heart; it is not just a statement. This is where people get confused. The whole

"I'm sorry," "I accept your apology" dance is often conducted without a second thought. Both comments are ingrained in our culture as the "right" things to do, but more often than not, they're just words. The act of forgiving may sometimes require much introspective effort and, other times, an outward confrontation. Sometimes the words are spoken, but the intentions aren't in agreement or vice versa. It varies from situation to situation and person to person.

EARLY

This is a very uncomfortable topic, but we have to go here. Most sexual experiences and abuse happen to children, and the primary participants are usually family members, close family friends, or neighbors. They are people who have unmonitored access and time. Through my interviewing process, time and time again, women mentioned the fact that their trauma came from other children. Children with changing bodies and raging hormones. Children with partially developed cerebral cortexes and limited perspective. Children who had either seen or experienced something themselves or were "experimenting." Although some may not initially consider these experiences to be a "big deal," these events could qualify as first experiences in your own "sex story."

Because this is an unsettling topic to discuss, people tend to become masters of suppression and denial. Over the years, the details become vague while the effects are lasting. *Was it five or 15 times? How long did it last? What exactly happened?* Sometimes the answers to these questions seem so far away. Then there are details that we can never forget, like the T.V. show that was on, the aroma in the air, or the scent of cologne or perfume. The darnedest details take up permanent residency in the mind of the victim. As a result of the abuse, the victim tends to be faced with several decisions. *Do I share, and how much? What difference will it make in the end?* Despite the impact of the abuse, the beginning of healing is for the victim to reach out and grab the power that the experience stole.

PART II: CONVERSATION CORNER

Now what

Ok ok, I'm convinced I should be talking about sex more, but where do I start?

• **Research the human body.** God's artwork of our bodies is truly masterful! Research the body and all of its functions—especially those related to sex. Instead of stumbling across bits of information, take a proactive role in actively seeking it.

• **Become self-aware.** Highlight the unique parts of you and your journey—both mental and physical. Identify how these aspects help or harm you. Plan to directly address both your strengths and weaknesses in more fruitful ways.

• **Refuse to be unheard.** Even if you choose not to speak, be empowered to reside there confidently, not because you feel you have no choice. However, if something tries to muzzle you or lock you into an unwanted silence, speak to it. Understand that you have power whether you're asserting it or not. Take inventory of the things that are in your power. Choose to make decisions as opposed to living a life dictated to you by circumstance.

GROUP SENTENCE STARTERS

Chapter 4: Blissful Ignorance	Chapter 5: Is this normal?	Chapter 6: Twisted Minds and Their Trails of Residue
"I don't deliberately seek out certain information about sex because…"	"When I feel like something isn't right with me in any capacity, I tend to…"	"When I think about the impact of sexual abuse, I want to…"

TREND BREAKERS

- What do you think are some of the biggest myths about sex, and what impact do you think they have had on society at large? On an individual basis, what can you do to address these things?
- **Challenge:** Assess your comfort level in talking about sex. Strike up a conversation with someone far more comfortable than you, and also someone a bit less comfortable than you. Assume the role of teacher and student. Ask: "What is something you wish you would've known?" and "Is there anything you'd like to know?"

PART III: WHEN WE START TO TALK ABOUT SEX...

CHAPTER 7: TURN ONS AND TURN OFFS

 The tides don't command the ship. The sailor does."

— OGWO DAVID EMENIKE

I n this conversation centered around sex, each individual has the opportunity to assess their own sexuality and their awareness or lack or awareness in relation to it. What I'm mainly referring to is "turn ons" and "turn offs". Although the light may appear to be green, that doesn't mean the car will always go.

Factors that serve as "turn ons" are things that cause arousal and freedom to be sexually conscious. It can be as simple as a sensory detail or as direct as actual physical contact. Adversely, "turn offs" are factors that may distract you or prevent your mind and body from being seduced or moved sexually. Being conscious of your turn-ons and turn-offs is vital in the process of intentionally facilitating optimum sexual opportunities.

HIS AND HER DRIVE

It's common to hear that men have a higher sex drive than women. While science historically attributed this idea to the fact that men, on average, produce far more testosterone than women, we now recognize other libido altering sources: mental, physical and spiritual. In other words, "the mood." The mood can be shifted in several different ways. The increase or decrease in libido function can be medical, mental, or both. So, if you have a sex drive that is high, low, or anywhere in between, fear not—chances are, it's more common than you think.

We've all seen movies and read books where the romantic scene makes us roll our eyes. Come on, guys, I get the intent, but often that stuff is cheesy.

> *"Where did he get access to a pontoon boat?"*
> *"How did he get fireworks to shoot out her name?"*

As cute as fiction may be, it doesn't quite push the gas for me. However, if my husband comes into the room and says, "Let me know when your movie goes off so I can vacuum," suddenly, the room gets hot. *Did someone turn up the thermostat?* I don't know why my mind works this way, and frankly, I couldn't care less. I lean in. What is he going to vacuum? Is it this room I'm in, or the entire house? Is he going to do the stairs too? Lord, is the house on *fire*? All jokes aside, I find that removing the environmental factors that press on my brakes is a turn on for me. Those factors include everything I have to, want to, or should be doing— from chores to parenting tasks and meal prep. If the path to getting those things done is made smoother or just removed completely, I find more mental space to feel, to desire, to be pleased. The more crap on my mental plate, the less room I make for fun—for the most part anyway.

FETISHES

While I described chores as a "hot spot" for me, there are many unique turn-ons out there. Some unique and less popular factors are known as fetishes. They are objects, body parts, fantasies that inspire extreme or abnormal sexual excitement. Though many fetishes are uncommon, it's important to note that they aren't all "bad". As long as they don't control you or cause you to sin, they may not work against you. Back in 1998, there was a movie called *There's Something About Mary* where one of the characters had a shoe fetish. This man sat in the middle of the floor in a pile of shoes and was having the time of his life. Although the movie was comically exaggerated, I thought, "I bet there are people out here who really do get off on shoes." While I had not heard of nor experienced any fetishes of my own, I later found out I was right. While a fetish itself is not a "bad" thing, without self-control or proper acknowledgment, it can lead people to make poor choices.

Maybe you have a fetish or are involved with someone who has one—or several. Think about it. Are there any items, objects, or body parts that particularly draw your interest? Some are more socially acceptable than others. Some are ingrained in culture, but if I drift into that topic, this chapter will never end. Don't think of it in just a "creepy" "*There's Something About Mary*" kind of way; it could be a simple "thing" you are often drawn to. Maybe it's the look or shape of certain body parts or items you think of when trying to set the atmosphere or mood. If a fetish is harmful or dangerous, it needs to be addressed, curbed, or completely removed. Adversely, certain fetishes can be incorporated safely into one's active sex-life. Perhaps the "shoe fetish guy" can request sex with shoes on or purchase shoes for his spouse to model for him. Either way, fetishes need to be pulled to the forefront of the conversation if they are present in order to directly address them and their impact on ones perspective and preferences.

What experiences with fetishes have you had or heard of? What do you think of when you hear the word fetish? Do you have any fetishes or strong preferences?

TURNOFFS

Imagine climbing the mountain of ecstasy, almost reaching the top, but being snatched down by your infant waking up crying to the top of her lungs. Some moms can continue to seal the deal and sign the contract...I'm not that mom. My focus is immediately shifted and I have to remove the new factor pressing on my brakes so I can continue to accelerate. So, there I am, not an ounce of clothing on breastfeeding in the dark—pissed. With the knowledge of my distractibility, I must make room for myself concerning my turn offs. I find that identifying my turn offs are a great way for me to access my turn-ons. The same could be true for you.

Anything that requests my time can serve as a turn-off or if I'm not intentionally maintaining my mental peace. Work, cooking, cleaning, family, friends, health, empathy, whatever the heck else jumps on the bandwagon, too. I sometimes will examine the load and find some random smurf or unicorn that has no business in there, and I shake my head in disbelief.

Why do we tend to invest in seemingly meaningless thoughts so often?

Furthermore, why do we allow these thoughts to impact our sex lives? Some of the loads we tote are just downright impossible to carry and maintain reasonable peace at the same time. These loads weren't actually meant to be carried simultaneously to begin with. You must decide what things matter most to you and shift the ranking of priority for said items. Yes, cooking dinner is important, but you may want to prioritize brushing your teeth first thing in the morning beforehand. While that's a lightweight example, I'm sure you catch my drift. If something is weighing particularly heavy on you, ask yourself how carrying that weight is serving you holistically. If it's not helping, find another place to direct your attention and intentions. I'm not asking you to take certain things off of your plate because the bottom line is, sometimes you can't! However, I am urging you to focus on prioritizing the items of highest importance first.

WHAT DO YOU LIKE?

In a particular session I hosted, a woman described in detail some of the issues she was encountering sexually. It all boiled down to her not being in the mood! The more we talked, the more we both realized therapy wouldn't be a bad idea to help her sort through her mental baggage. More than that, we learned she didn't know what her turn-ons were. Without taking a breath, she was able to ramble off eighteen million kajillion things that turn her off:

"He sweats heavy."
"He says 'this.'"
"He doesn't say 'that.'"
"He...he...he...he...he."

Once the air fully escaped her lungs, and she drew her first breath, I asked, "Well, what do you like?" She started describing things she didn't like to help her explain. I stopped her again, restating my question: "What do you like though?" It wasn't that she didn't hear or understand the question; the fact of the matter was ... she didn't know. Can you describe what you like? Furthermore, can you identify why?

UNLEASH THE FREAK

Traditionally, men are the perceived "pursuers," and women are the "pursued." Under that mindset, you'll find several hidden and potentially harmful mindsets: "Men are supposed to do 'X,' and women aren't supposed to do 'Y.'" When it comes to sex and conversations about it, it's not abnormal for a woman to play coy. However, stepping out of that mindset can be the key to producing new and beautiful layers to your sex life. You don't have to wait for your needs to be met or desires to be addressed; it's your life, and sex is a participatory sport. Don't just "lie" there. Give yourself permission to open up and truly enjoy.

You deserve to be available to conceive of all things conducive to your mental, spiritual and physical well-being, and part of that is actively identifying and removing barriers that try to hinder that. You must play an active role in your enjoyment!

CHAPTER 8: SENSUALITY

 "The noblest pleasure is the joy of understanding."

— LEONARDO DA VINCI

The pace of life can seem so swift. We come and go, often without taking the time to simply "smell the roses." It isn't until something interrupts the flow that we're even made mindful of just how much life we're truly allowing to pass us by. Interruptions as simple as misplacing keys or a remote can slow us down just enough to force us to be a little more analytical about our desires, needs, and overall mental state. Routines in life can be beneficial, making day to day tasks more efficient, but they can also rob us of unique opportunities to activate all of our senses. Sensuality is the ability to physically use your senses to navigate, explore, and enhance aspects of your life and surroundings. While discussing our mental "feelings" is a more familiar process, investigating what we are physically "feeling" may be a bit more infrequent. It's a precious gift that can complement life—if you allow it to.

"Stop and smell the roses" is a phrase I've heard time and time again without actually giving much thought to its literal meaning. When I was younger, my mother had quite a green thumb. In addition to cultivating several thriving gardens, she planted a rose bush right beside the front porch of our childhood home. It grew and presented itself beautifully year after year. I remember how mesmerized I was by the gorgeous velvety petals. We were proud of what it did for the curb appeal of our home. I would get lost in the very essence of that bush, ripping off petals, pricking my fingers on the thorns, and even tearing off a flower or two to take with me because I didn't want the moment to end. Even now, I can get lost in the appreciation of that memory. I realize I don't always devote much time to simply allowing myself to indulge in the beauty that my senses make available.

Which of the five senses do you think people use most often during sex (in addition to physical touch, of course)? Which sense is your favorite? How often do you deliberately engage your senses for pleasure? Which of your senses do you use most/least frequently and why?

Senses are powerful! The sense of taste, touch, smell, sight, and sound all serve unique yet similar purposes; they help us assess our surroundings. With the information collected from our senses, we can make decisions to assist us in many ways, including accomplishing goals, protecting us from potentially harmful situations, and just plain feeling good. If one sense is lacking or absent, the others intensify to help the person explore the world around them. Likewise, our senses are key tools in accessing pleasure. Think about it, beyond the mental and spiritual aspects, all physical pleasure is directly attached to your senses. Even our dreams are coated with sensory details.

Armed with this in mind, how acclimated are you with intentionally using yours?

SMELL

Imagine walking by a bakery, and the scent of fresh-baked something or other drifts out and smacks you in the face. The smell is so enticing that your mouth starts watering almost immediately. Food wasn't even on your mind as you had a list of other priorities, but the aroma that just confronted you has momentarily shifted your focus. You close your eyes and lose yourself in the fragrance, and just like that, you decide to buy the first pastry you can get your hands on (and you weren't even hungry). That's a non-intentional example of your sense of smell influencing your behavior for pure enjoyment. An intentional example would be lighting a scented candle or putting on an aromatic oil or fragrance. Activating the sense of smell is a great way to enhance "the mood." The Bible was all about that scent life. Frankincense and Myrrh seemed to be the go-to as well as other delightful smelling plants and herbs for both health and recreational benefits[1].

Frankincense and Myrrh are gummy substances derived from the sap of Boswellia and Commophora trees. [6]They are used for various purposes but most commonly recognized for their distinctive aromas. In the Bible, myrrh is used in combination with other oils to "purify" and enhance the beauty of Queen Esther (Esther 2:12) They were also brought to infant Jesus as gifts by one of the Magi (Matthew 2:11).

Your sense of smell can also deter your path, like sniffing sour milk can prevent you from taking a sip, or unexpectedly smelling smoke can make you check for fire.

SIGHT

Is there anything more visually appealing than nature itself? The way the leaves wave at the subtle kiss of the wind. The response of a body of water to drops of rain like tears from the sky, making small but rippling impressions as they meet the surface. The glow of fire as it jumps and dances to the rhythm of its own beat. Some sights are just satisfying beyond what we can seem to explain.

What sights in nature do you enjoy seeing? Are there any other visuals that stand out to you in a positive way?

What we see and appreciate in comparison to what we're comfortable displaying or showing is an interesting conversation within itself. In many religious circles, the idea of "modesty" is a hot topic. It's a hot topic because what it means to be "modest" varies depending on location, community and often individual opinion. Some people regard "showing skin" as lacking modesty, while others may evaluate "skin showage" on a case-by-case basis. Factors like height, body type, and overall confidence can make an article of clothing look vastly different from one person to the next. This is complicated because individuals with identical behaviors are often regarded differently by their physique. Being called more or less "Godly" or "modest" based on moving targets can get very complicated to navigate, teach or even explain by these standards.

Part of looking and feeling sexy has a lot to do with how one feels about his or her own appearance—self-esteem. What aspects of your physical body are you most proud of? Adversely, what areas could stand a bit of improvement? I've found that maximizing your strengths is a great place to start to improve how you feel about yourself. Regarding your physical body: you may not like your stomach, but you love your boobs. So, don't wear clothes that make your stomach the focal point. You may want to wear shirts that accentuate your breast and just kind of flow at the stomach. If you love your eyes maybe you choose to wear contact lenses instead of glasses. There are lots of choices that are within your power to address.

It's natural to admire beauty. We all can marvel at the wonders of God's works. Like a beautiful sunset to a rolling river, we can all pick and choose aspects that resonate with us, and those aspects may differ from person to person. Likewise, we can admire people, their physiques and their choices of adornment to accent the characteristics they value most about themselves. As young children we look at the adults in our visual reach and consider the aspects we want to duplicate and avoid. The conflict comes in when the opportunity to converse about appearance and attire are squelched and people develop feelings of unnecessary insecurity or rebellion.

What factors do you consider when choosing clothing? When it comes to seeing yourself, what aspects of your physical appearance do you like most? Which aspects do you like least? What aspects of a man's appearance do you appreciate the most and why?

HEARING

Sounds can both lure and repel us in various ways. Mellow low tones are pleasing to hear. This is why instruments like the bass can carry a tune like none other. It's why moaning can somehow make childbirth easier, or why humming can lull a baby to sleep. Sounds like heavy breathing and moans can also enhance arousal as they can be associated with unarticulated pleasure and sincere enjoyment. Sounds are conducive to communication and accessing a relaxed state. Likewise, the sound of a siren or the "ouch" sound (you know the sound of sucking in air between clenched teeth) can make you freeze immediately. It is said that music is one of the only things that can enter your consciousness without your permission. That is powerful!

Manipulating the sounds you hear can grant you the opportunity to shift the atmosphere for yourself and anyone else present. Upbeat fast tempo music can motivate movement, this would be good for working out or cleaning. Likewise, music with a slower tempo can encourage calmness. This would be good for relaxing and preparing for rest. If you're feeling chaotic or anxious, take inventory of the sounds surrounding you. You may want to remove some auditory distractions or remove yourself from an environment to stabilize yourself. This may look like leaving a room, taking a walk or simply changing your physical location or access point.

In terms of sex, consider how sound impacts you and entertain the idea of using it to enhance your pleasure. Take a moment to consider, what sounds can you incorporate into your day to day life to increase your pleasure?

TOUCH

The human body is a galaxy of a whole lot of stuff—skin, muscles, bones, nerve endings and a bunch of other stuff sprawled about the entire body and interacting in ways I can't begin to explain nor fully understand. This helps that, and that works with this. You know the song, *"The knee bones connected to the..thigh bone."* Where do we even begin? When it comes to physical touch, especially sexually, the art of observation and communication are essential for optimum pleasure. There's no one size fits all shoe in this department.

One day, I was at the park with my daughter, and I kicked off my sandals to relax as I sat on the grass. When I stood up, I noted how soft the grass felt on the soles of my feet. This must've been some premium level grass or something because it felt amazing! There were no rocks or sticks nearby, and the grass itself felt almost cottony if I could try to describe it. Anyway, I figured my baby would get a kick out of feeling the sensation on her feet, too. I lifted her from the blanket and lowered her to the point where her feet and the grass met. She was not enthused, as she immediately snatched her feet up from the ground. The lower I descended her body, the higher her legs raised up. Clearly, the sensation I felt didn't do it for her like it did for me. The same touch that sends one person on a euphoric high, can send another on a disgusted retreat. This is relevant sexually because if you aren't aware, you may unintentionally subject or be subjected to someone else's idea of pleasure. I can't tell you the countless times women have described their partners "go to" moves that just don't do it for them. Their intent is to provide the pleasurable sensation that they get from the act, but it means little to nothing if the recipient can't relate nor find the words to explain.

Can you think of a texture or non-sexual touch that is pleasurable to you? Is there a particular feeling that most people like that you don't? Is there a particular sensation that you like and others may not? How many ways can you think of incorporating seemingly non-sexual feelings into sexual acts?

> Try this: Raise your eyebrows. Did your ears move? Can you move your eyebrows without causing your ears to move? The same way your ears and eyebrows move together, there are other body part relationships that function that way without us being fully conscious of them. Being aware of the way your body functions in pronounced and subtle ways is key in achieving optimal physical pleasure.

The adventure of learning about the human body should be met with excitement and an open mind, especially concerning physical touch in tandem with mental stimulation. Physical touch is unique because you can use your entire body to experience it. While hearing is exclusive to your ears, smelling to your nose and so on and so forth, your sense of touch can be accessed from the very hair follicles on your head down to the soles of your feet and everywhere in between.

TASTE

Contrary to popular belief, the taste buds on your tongue aren't the only things that allow you to taste. There are taste cells on the back of your throat, in your nose and sinus, and even your epiglottis (the little hanging thing in the back of your throat).[2] The experience of tasting is unique because it can be beneficial for enjoyment as well as protection. It causes you to enjoy a delightful flavor and likewise informs you that something may be harmful or dangerous. It's important to note that your sense of taste can evolve over time. The dreadful taste of certain veggies to the child version of myself are now part of some of my most desired meals. Some flavors appeal most to certain times, seasons or activities. Adding pleasurable flavors to less desirable objects can, in turn, cause that item to be desired. This is why we season our food and add sugars and salt to processed foods. Familiarity also aids us in the appreciation for certain flavors. Culturally some spices and seasonings are commonplace for some that are not even available in other communities. Pleasurable flavors can impact how you feel and think, use flavor and taste to enhance your mood thus strengthening your access to pleasure.

ALTOGETHER

When considering the sensory experience of life and its influence on our ability to take part in physical pleasure, it's important to be conscious of ourselves, our preferences, and our desires.

What do you like? Can you articulate what feels good to you? If you don't know, how can you expect to communicate it to someone else?

Think about it this way, we are all familiar with feeling "bad" or having a "bad day." If we were more in tune with the power of our senses, we could utilize them more to enhance or compliment our moods and overall emotional responses in various situations. This is part of what makes certain vices enticing to some. People generally just want to feel "good." I'm not suggesting that your sensory experience will fix all of life's troubles, but I am saying heightened awareness of your senses can bear a significant impact in one's life.

> Try This: Dragging through day-to-day life following a routine can be exhausting. Work, Eat, sleep—work, eat, sleep—what if you deliberately engaged all your senses daily for your pleasure. What would that look like for you? **Make a list of ways you can use your senses to heighten your day, try to add things that you've never done before.**

When it comes to sex and conversations about it, I can't stress enough how familiarizing oneself with what feels good will enhance your personal experience. Without this consciousness and understanding, some people forfeit their opportunities to grow. I can't tell you the countless times I've interacted with women who continue to entangle themselves with men sexually because of the man's expertise. Single, saved, and married alike—these women live lives devoid of developing awareness of their own pleasure, so a simple look or a handshake from a suitor is judgment-altering to them. The visual of the eye contact and physical touch of a hand can carry them through the roof. Girl, that man is about to wreck your life in one swoop, but you can't see it because you can't quite identify why he's so alluring. In that same breath, people are quick to "fall out of love" or not be attracted to their spouses anymore for that same sentiment. Not getting enough sensual activation or too much undesirable sensation can cause one to flee! Now there are many contributing factors, and I'm not going to disrespect them, but I can say that losing consciousness or lessening the frequency of the "feel good factors" can certainly contribute to this situation as well.

Lean into and learn about the sensations that feel good to you! Strengthen your awareness and familiarity with your body.

Ask yourself: What do I like?

If you can't answer that question to yourself, take some time and seek out the answers.

CHAPTER 9: BEYOND YOUR WILDEST DREAMS

 The single raindrop never feels responsible for the flood"

— DOUGLAS ADAMS

There is a sweet spot located right on the edge of science, faith, and sheer will power and effort. It is the place where facts and supposed fiction have a stand-off, and pure bliss resides. In this place is where the norm is challenged, where individuality is born. This is the home of the ultimate, most euphoric experience(s)—oh, and great sex! Think of the best possible physical and/or mental experience you can conceive of, now conceptualize the fact that there's even more beyond that...and it's accessible to you! The problem is that we don't often entertain that probability which thereof hinders its likelihood of ever even occurring in most cases. If it does by chance occur, we are not usually cultured or equipped to duplicate it on our own terms within the frame of our intentional lifestyles, moral compasses and frame of logic.

Basically, if we stumble up on something specific, we may or may not know it or what to do with it.

Anatomically speaking, there are several physical features and biological parts of our bodies whose only identifiable purpose is for pleasure. Scientists have studied human anatomy and sexuality earlier than our oldest known written records can speak to, and still there is more beauty and revelation unfolding day by day. Sex is an art form that can be researched and recorded, but the most informational aspect of it is the experience of the individual. Understanding the individual experience is pertinent because there are just as many (if not more) factors that can prevent or restrict the pleasurable aspects of the experience as well.

BROADENING THE SCOPE

Great sex is not a birth right, it's an opportunity. That's right! I said it! Penetration is basic, in and out-in and out. You get the picture. It's important to note that penetration is merely a portion of the experience. The entire act encompasses far more mental and spiritual involvement than is often recognized. When you think about sex, what do you focus on? Try this, take penetration out of the picture...what then are you left with? Often times people inflate the idea of penetration so much when thinking of sex, that a lot of the God given beauty is zapped from their vantage point. From that place, what was meant to be an enriching, enhancing, euphoric vacation can sometimes get interpreted as a time consuming inconvenience. People tend to be far more "busy" in their day to day lives to even take notice of all that's happening with one another. During sex, there is usually an agreement to pay attention. Being in such close proximity demands attention both intentionally and unintentionally. Attention to ourselves, our partners and our surroundings. Here is an important note: pay attention! Devote your conscious mind to the positive and pleasurable aspects of the act. This will shift the experience greatly if you're not already doing this. With every opportunity you get, build on what you have already discovered in order to maintain, adjust and ultimately improve. Any great lover can testify that they have grown significantly over time.

DIVE INTO THE DETAILS

Imagine being served a world famous 5-star meal. I mean, it's not that everyone else thinks this meal is good, it is by far the absolute best composition of food and flavor. It's legitimately stellar! You take the plate, smell it, admire the presentation and even lean in to hear the sizzle as the deliciousness responds to its recent fling on the stove. You take pictures and compliment the chef...but you have yet to actually taste it. You merely appreciate it for what it is. Right? Sex is very similar to that plate in many ways. As beautiful as it is, there is still more to the story. There's always more to the story! The best movies make you wonder about the characters long after the credits roll. As wonderful as it is to behold this plate as your own, you have to pick up the fork and dive in! Eat!

Aside from pregnancy and organ donation, sex is the closest that 2 individuals could ever physically be. It is a layered engagement that supersedes the act itself. A lot of people feel like mind-blowing sex is supposed to just happen with little to no effort despite life's circumstances. While it happens, it's not always the case. A thriving sex life requires priority, willingness, and for you to own your sexuality and the foundation on which it stands! One should be actively involved in the maintenance and adjustments that go into sustaining a healthy and balanced perspective, which ultimately supports a healthy sex life. What was once required to get "in the mood" in youth may not be a factor as we age and mature.

THE BIG O

I'm sure you've been waiting for this section, and I'll try my best not to disappoint. An orgasm can be summarized as the climax of sexual excitement, the peak of pleasure, a crown of the royal head, if you will. It is the result of maximized enjoyment. Like traveling by plane, train, and taxi cab, there are different ways to get there, so let's start there.

> What happens during an orgasm?
> Some things that often occur during orgasms: -increased heart rate, -increased pulse, -increased production of bodily secretions, -permissive involuntary movements, -increased blood flow, -rhythmic contractions of the muscles, -increased body temperature

While familiarizing yourself with a pleasurable sensation can initiate the ride toward an orgasm, manipulation of multiple pleasure principles can accelerate the process. It's important to note that in addition to physical acts, your mental state holds a significant amount of responsibility in your access to optimal sexual pleasure. Perspective is everything! I'm not going to lie, climaxing without physical touch is an impressive feat that many may never experience —but it can be done!

Orgasm time lengths vary for different people and in different ways. Before we get to the numbers, I think it's important to note that both medical and mental health professionals define orgasm differently.[1] This was a significant finding to me! I had to figure out the difference between their views and mine to examine what I had previously known. Then I had to decide if I needed to revamp my opinions for the sake of relaying the information to others more accurately. It also made me challenge the foundation of all the conversations I've had about sex and orgasms (both formal interviews and informal). Were we talking about the same things? I wonder what the people I had previously spoken to actually thought or knew. This screws up all my poor little data in terms of accuracy, but not in terms of perception.

> Medical professionals define orgasm by the physiological factors. Psychologists and mental health professionals tend to define orgasm by emotional and cognitive factors. Simply put: there isn't one absolute definition as to what an orgasm is, but there are certain similarities amongst the findings.

THE EROGENOUS ZONES

There are whole books, studies, and dissertations written specifically about the erogenous zones of our bodies. Erogenous zones are super sensitive parts of the body. They are usually nooks and crannys, but also commonly "ticklish" places. While there are several obviously popular ones, there are also some less popular yet significant ones that serve us well in terms of pleasure. It's important to note that these zones can be different for men and women. Here is a short list of some erogenous zones of the female body:

- scalp
- ears
- lips
- neck
- shoulders
- armpits
- wrists
- joint creases (all of them)
- breast (nipples included of course)
- stomach
- buttocks (anus included)
- vaginal region (all of it)
- feet
- toes

Maybe at some point I'll write a book specifically on this topic because there are so many more bullets that can be noted and even more information to share about them, but I figured I'd just list a snippet. The main point I'm trying to drive home is that there is more to consider when it comes to "feeling good" aside from the traditional and most common locations. "If it can tickle, it may cause a trickle" if you know what I mean. Some sensations may be significantly more pleasurable than others. If you increase your awareness of these zones and their effects, you have created the opportunity to deliberately increase the quality of your sexual experiences and mature without exerting as much energy. You can then communicate these findings successfully with your partner who can in turn present you with new opportunities and ideas to consider.

Sometimes a partner is more aware of the manipulation of the erogenous zones than you are. In society, men are oftentimes granted a lot more sexual grace and empowerment than women. Even if they aren't "acting" on the information they obtain, there seems to be less resistance and taboo toward them obtaining said information. To simply "feel good" as a man, can be just that. However, with women "feeling good" is rationalized differently. Time and time again I've heard that men can "cheat" and it not mean as much because it was just "sex". Have you heard that one before? If not, let me explain. The common idea is that a man doesn't have to have much of connection with a woman at all to have sex with her. However, a woman is expected to act and live at such a distance with her sexuality and discretion that it is viewed "worse" when a woman cheats. They say that a woman has to care and be involved in a way that isn't typically required if a man were to commit the same act. I know of situations where this is both true and not. The reality is that the act is the same. Period. But our perception depends on the layers and circumstances and all of these things must be taken into consideration when evaluating an occurrence. The bottom line is that there is a popular distinction in how men and women usually go about learning about sexuality in general and all that connects to it.

ROADBLOCKS

It's important to note that some things can get "in the way" of your intended sexual thoughts, conversations, and purposes. For example, there is some local construction being done in the neighborhood and while it doesn't have to stop me from going places it may shift how I get there. If I know that a street is blocked for through traffic, then I won't drive that direction. If it's significantly noisy at a certain time

I won't plan to put the kids down for a nap. If I'm giving someone directions on how to navigate getting to my location, I have to be very descriptive and more than likely take them "out of the way" just to arrive, but as long as they get to me then it doesn't even matter. When it comes to sex and conversations about it, you have to incorporate the information you have about your specific "roadblocks" into your plan so they don't work against you. Weight, height, and shape alone can deem certain sex positions impossible for some. Self esteem and the "season of life" play huge roles in this regard.

During the process of interviewing women for this book, I learned some fascinating and effective ways around these factors. Take inventory of yourself and your physical and mental capabilities.

What specific factors about you and your life may require additional creativity when it comes to sex?

If you have bad knees, obviously, you shouldn't be the one trying to "drop it like it's hot." Likewise, if you're insecure about certain aspects of yourself, you should consider confronting or addressing those insecurities before you allow them to rob you of the fullness of the sexual experiences that are possible for you. Now some insecurities can't be "fixed", and I'm not necessarily suggesting that you "fix" them, but I am requiring you to "fix" your mindsets toward them.

HYPE YOURSELF UP

The "boss" is known for usually being the one making the decisions. They can set the tone. They can delegate tasks and empower decision making. You need to give yourself permission to be the "boss" in terms of what you choose to and not to do concerning your body. Aside from the one that created you, you are the boss of your body and mind. Long before you involve yourself with anyone else, you exist. You must make choices that empower you to access your greatest potential. Before the actual "doing" part of having sex there is the mental component that you must take an active role in.

CREATE A VIBE

Here are some of the things you can do to shift your mindset and overall well-being. You can also use these items as talking points in conversation.

• **Affirm yourself:** Your mental narrative needs to support positive self-consciousness. Speak positive affirmations over yourself ("I'm sexy." "I'm beautiful." "There's no one on this earth quite like me."). Do you affirm yourself? How often? What are some of your favorite affirmations?

• **Breathe:** Take time to simply breathe. You can do this anytime and anywhere. You're literally doing it right now! It costs you nothing to slow down and center yourself, so do it more intentionally. Take slow, deep breaths. In your breathing moments, think on good things. Pray. Meditate. How often do you pause and just breathe? Go ahead, take a deep breath...right now!

- **Spruce yourself up:** Looking good can make you feel good, so do something with yourself! Dress up, get your hair done/try a wig, get your eyebrows arched. See the version of yourself that appears with the help of your effort. The world around you will change the way it responds to you when you deliberately show up! People will start affirming you via compliments and pleasant interactions, you can then roll this vibe into the affirmations you tell yourself. This will create a cycle. You'll even start to look at yourself differently. What does it look like for you to "spruce yourself up"? What are your "go-to's"? What do you refuse to do and why? How is this working for you?

- **Stay ready:** If you feel like you're unprepared to "show up" in any capacity, this will be the breeding ground for insecurity and missed opportunities. Shower, wear cute panties (or no panties), moisturize your skin. What small moves and practices can you implement to "stay ready"?

- **Try something new:** You're used to what you're used to. Take a moment and deliberately try something new. New food. New drink. New position. Try something different— you may like it. Keep in mind, everything you do is a result of you trying something new at some point. Use that thought to combat your reservations or fear. Have fun and allow yourself to enjoy life. Routines can sometimes drain the life out of you. Allow yourself to smile and find things that make you feel good. What's something new that you can try today? What has prevented you from trying new things? How can you try something new without it causing too much of an inconvenience? When trying something new also consider having a plan for if it doesn't turn out the way you expected (i.e., a backup plan). If you're trying a new entree for example, you may want to choose familiar and delicious sides. You may also prepare to order something else in the event that it's disgusting so you don't end up hungry and disappointed.

• **Keep good company:** Surrounding yourself with supportive and uplifting people will impact your outlook for the better. Roll some of that positive energy into your sex life. If you can't think of anyone or no one is available, use the internet. Pick up the phone, follow positive people on social media, listen to life-affirming podcasts and streams. Who are some positive people you would like to spend more time with? What makes you consider these people "good company"?

• **Be good company:** There are certain aspects of our personalities that make being around us enjoyable for different people. Adversely, there are also some repelling factors within us as well. Maximize the life-giving aspects of yourself; they will attract people who are looking for the energy you provide. What is your favorite aspect of your personality? What do people say they like most about you? What would you hope people would say they like most about you? What aspect of your personality serves as the biggest threat to your strongest attributes?

• **Compliment others:** Say kind things. Get used to hearing yourself affirm others. This will give you familiarity with making people feel good, and you can use this in the bedroom for "dirty talk." It can be something as simple as an affirming pleasurable moan to a full fledged statement or stream of statements. Don't say anything you're uncomfortable with or awkward about. Keep it true and keep it simple if you need to. What types of compliments are easiest for you to give? Are there any compliments that are difficult for you to say? Why?

• **Drink some water:** It's no secret, the majority of your body is made up of water. You need it! Your vagina needs it. Your mouth produces saliva, your eyes produce tears, you sweat from your pores, and don't forget you pee daily. Water is leaving your body all the time; it would serve you well to deliberately take some in. How much water do you drink on average?

More than half of the US population is chronically dehydrated. It's so bad that many peoples thirst mechanism isn't functioning correctly, and people actually confuse thirst for hunger. This is a great contributor to overeating and the ever-growing obesity rate.

LET THE CONVERSATION BEGIN

The fact of the matter is that sex is a well-spring of opportunity and conversations about it should be rich and plentiful. In society, we should talk about it much more and feel comfortable while doing it, and that starts with each of us. These conversation can in turn significantly reduce the burdens of sexual abuse as more people will have access and liberty to talk about their experiences. Relationships and marriages can and will be strengthened as women become more familiar with their voice overall, but especially concerning this topic. Intentionally engaging in these conversations will change lives, for the better! We all need to be more aware of the roles we play in each other's lives in general.

Sex is far too loud in this day and age to be so silenced conversationally, and its getting louder! May these conversations and the information in this book grant us the tools necessary to navigate some of the complexities that hinder us in order to experience the ecstasy that awaits. Armed with new perspective and empowerment to make adjustments for yourself and others, make the commitment to talk about sex and the Complexities of Ecstasy in an empowered and proactive way.

PART III: CONVERSATION CORNER

Now what:

Now that I'm more aware of the fact that we don't talk about sex enough, what should I do? Where do I go from here?

• **Never stop growing and learning!** If you realize that you could stand a little more "sex talk" in your life, start by asking questions. Before you speak to someone else, you have to formulate the ideas. Sometimes we possess more knowledge than we think. Think of broad ideas and concepts that you could stand to learn a little more about, then zoom in to more personal inquiries about your own life, body, and experiences. Simply ask yourself: why?

• **Identify any areas of your life where you've been untruthful—both consciously and unconsciously—and make a plan to address them.** What adjustments can you make to live in truth? In the age of growing social media and access to digital content, what impact has pornography and media beauty standards had on me and/or my immediate social community?

• **Find your voice.** Whether your voice is loud and booming or quiet and restrained, there is a whole lifetime of development that contributes to it being what it is. Take a moment and examine how you got the voice that you have and if you want to keep it the same or make adjustments that serves you better.

GROUP SENTENCE STARTERS

Chapter 7: Turn ons and Turn offs	Chapter 8: Sensuality	Chapter 9: Beyond your wildest dreams
"Taking control and asserting myself makes me feel..."	"A sensation that feels surprisingly good to me is..."	"I know there are possibilities beyond my current reality. I want to experience more, but..."

TREND BREAKERS

- Physically loosen up! Relax your shoulders, roll your neck, and unclench your jaw. Schedule an appointment for a massage--regularly. Its not just for luxury, its purposeful to get used to feeling good regularly outside of sexual acts. Allow yourself to loosen up for the sake of loosening up. You deserve it, and it'll give you better access to clearer thoughts.
- Get your blood flowing! Deliberately involve yourself in some sort of physical activity today. If doing a full out workout regimen is too much for you, then start out simply stretching or walking and build from there.